THE SERPENT'S EGG

ALSO BY INGMAR BERGMAN

SCENES FROM A MARRIAGE
FACE TO FACE

DATE			

THE SERPENT'S EGG

A Film by

Ingmar Bergman

Translated from the Swedish by Alan Blair

*"Man is an abyss and I turn giddy
when I look down into it."*

GEORG BÜCHNER

PANTHEON BOOKS
New York

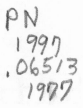

Library of Congress Cataloging in Publication Data
Bergman, Ingmar, 1918–
The Serpent's Egg.
Translation of *Ormens ägg*.
I. Title.
PN1997.06513   1977   791.43'7   77–3032
ISBN 0–394–41358–X
ISBN 0–394–73374–6 pbk.

The photographs throughout this book were taken
by Lars Looschen.

Manufactured in the United States of America

FIRST AMERICAN EDITION

THE SERPENT'S EGG

1

The scene is Berlin. It is late in the evening of Saturday, November 3, 1923, and a cutting wind blows through the badly lighted Albertstrasse, which extends through the endless district southwest of the abattoirs. A pack of cigarettes costs thirteen million marks, and ordinary people have largely lost faith in both the present and the future.

ABEL ROSENBERG is on his way home, rather drunk. He half runs—the summer overcoat is thin and affords little protection from the wind.

The boardinghouse is in a narrow cul-de-sac. The dining room on the third floor is full of people. A family party is in full swing—shouts, laughter, and dance music. A strong but unfamiliar smell of cooking forces its way out of the kitchen, where the landlady, FRAU HEMSE, is preparing supper together with her friends.

ABEL takes his key from the board at the reception desk, which has been deserted for the evening; goes quickly up the four flights; turns a corner; passes a short corridor smelling of coal fumes and the privy; fumbles for the keyhole; and enters the room.

The overhead light is on. It is a faintly glowing carbon-filament bulb under a porcelain shade with a beaded fringe. ABEL's brother, MAX, is sitting on the unmade bed. He has shot himself through the mouth. The back of his head is blown to pieces. Blood and brains are spattered over the bed and wall. He

3

is leaning backward, his eyes half closed and his mouth open. He is still holding the big army pistol in a tight grip. The noise and music can be heard from the dining room below.

2

The local police station the next day, Sunday, November 4. A pallid autumn sun filters through the dirty windows, which look out onto a yard with a few leafless trees.

INSPECTOR BAUER *enters, yawning and holding a mug of coffee. He is a fat, broad-shouldered man with red hair and a beard.*

ABEL *stands up at once and puts out a hand, which the inspector pretends not to see. He sits down behind the desk with his back to* ABEL *and sips his coffee as he watches some children playing in the yard. The coal fire in the corner emits a stifling heat.*

A female secretary now appears. She gives a curt nod to ABEL *and sits down, ready with pad and pencil. She is about forty, with shingled hair, and no makeup. The immaculately white blouse fits tightly across a pair of maternally swelling breasts.*

The inspector swivels round on his chair, puts down the mug with a slight slam, and looks impatiently at ABEL.

BAUER   So you don't speak German at all.

(ABEL *shakes his head*)

BAUER   Damned nuisance. Fräulein Dorst has had her Sunday ruined.

(Indicates the secretary)

ABEL   I'm sorry.

BAUER   What's your name?

ABEL   Abel Rosenberg. I'm thirty-five and was born in Canada of Danish parents. My brother, Max; his wife, Manuela; and I came to Berlin a month ago—no, it was the end of September. Max had hurt his wrist, so we couldn't perform any more. We're circus artists. We did a trapeze act.

(BAUER stares down at his cigar case, in which are two cigars, one whole and one half smoked. FRÄULEIN DORST doodles on her shorthand pad. BAUER lights the half-smoked cigar and puffs at it)

BAUER   Was there any reason for your brother's suicide? Depression? Unhappy love affair? Alcoholism? Drugs? Nervous breakdown? Fed up with life in general?

ABEL   I don't know.

BAUER   An unaccountable impulse, in other words? Oh, well, it happens. Did you get in touch with his wife?

ABEL   I tried last night and again this morning but couldn't get hold of her.

BAUER   Didn't all of you live together?

ABEL   No. Manuela and Max got divorced two years ago. When we were dismissed from the circus, Manuela started working at a cabaret. I'll go to see her this afternoon. The cabaret opens at three o'clock on Sundays.

BAUER May I see your papers, as a matter of form?

ABEL Here you are.

BAUER Thank you. *(Looking at the papers)* How are you going to pay for the funeral?

ABEL We've saved a little money.

BAUER Good. *(Casually)* You're Jewish?

ABEL Why?

BAUER Oh, nothing. I was just curious, Herr Rosenberg. *(Handing back the passport)* We can regard the interrogation as concluded. What are your plans?

(ABEL shrugs; says nothing)

BAUER How long will you stay in Berlin?

ABEL I'm not sure.

BAUER As you know, there is great unemployment. We don't like to see foreigners coming here and taking the few jobs that are available.

ABEL Yes, I know.

BAUER Our poor relief is badly strained after the war. We've no intention of taking care of you when your money runs out.

ABEL No, I know.

BAUER　Good-bye, Herr Rosenberg.

ABEL　Good-bye, Inspector. Good-bye, Fräulein Dorst.

3

After the interrogation, ABEL *heads directly to the restaurant where he usually has dinner. The time is one thirty; a raw mist has risen from the river; the bells of the nearby St. Elizabeth boom above the empty, endless streets.*

ABEL *hears footsteps behind him. Without turning around he begins to walk more quickly, but his pursuer catches up with him and puts his hand under* ABEL*'s arm. A worn face, with a large nose and heavy bags under the sharp, dark eyes, is turned toward* ABEL.

HOLLINGER　In a hell of a hurry, aren't you? Are you going to have dinner? So am I. It's on me. How are things, my dear Abel? And how are Max and Manuela? Do you think his wrist will soon be better? We miss you all, you know. The circus needs you. I suppose you're wondering what I'm doing here in Berlin when the circus is in Amsterdam. I'm looking for new acts, my boy. Nowadays I can get any damned stars I like, since they all know I pay in dollars. We're playing to full houses all the time. I could have a tent twice as big as the one I have now, and it would still be full.

(They enter the restaurant, which at this time of day is quite crowded. It is a comparatively high-class place with visible relics of bygone imperial luxury. Some musicians in greasy

tails are playing a languorous waltz behind a few palms. The headwaiter and waiters immediately flock around HOLLIN-GER *and his guest. They are shown to a table in an alcove, the walls of which are decorated with stained red silk and pictures of lewd women. A broken bracket lamp with a couple of sleepy bulbs sheds a warm glow over the table with its thick, clean but frayed linen cloth. A pungent smell of damp mold battles successfully with the reek of food and tobacco smoke.* HOLLINGER *orders vegetable soup and roast hare, the only dishes on the Sunday menu that inspire confidence, a bottle of schnapps in a cooler, and two mugs of beer)*

HOLLINGER   People need their circus. Everything has gone to the dogs. There's nothing to hold on to. Look what I read in the paper this morning. I'll try to translate it, as you don't know German.

(HOLLINGER *takes out the Saturday edition of* Völkischer Beobachter, *hunts for a few moments, then finds the place, which he has marked in pencil*)

HOLLINGER   Listen to this. *(Reads aloud)* "Terrible times are at hand when circumcised anti-Christian Asiatics on all sides are lifting their gory hands to strangle us. The massacre of Christians by the Jew Isaskar Zederblum, alias Mr. Lenin, was enough to make a Genghis Khan blush. A Jewish terrorist pack, trained to murder and assault, is prowling through the country, butchering honest citizens and farmers on transportable gallows."

(HOLLINGER *stops reading and peers at* ABEL *over his glasses, which have slipped to the end of his narrow, hooked nose. He smiles with thin lips and decayed yellow teeth.* ABEL, *who has quickly become drunk, meets his eyes uncomprehendingly.* HOLLINGER *scans the article lower down and finds what he is looking for*)

HOLLINGER   *(Reading)*   "Do you want first to see thousands of people hanging from lampposts in your town? Do you want to wait until a bolshevik commission starts its murderous work in your town just as in Russia? Do you want to stumble over the bodies of your women and children?"

(Once again HOLLINGER *looks searchingly at his friend, the circus artist. Getting no reaction, he reads the last sentence of the article*)

HOLLINGER *(Reading)* "Existence today seems to be nothing else but being full of dread."

Do you need money? I can lend you some. Look, here's six hundred million. Take them. I don't need them. I'm going back to Amsterdam tomorrow, and there's no point in changing them. I won't get anything for them anyway. I was in Munich on Thursday. There's talk of revolution, a revolution from the right, my dear Abel.

*(*HOLLINGER *smiles again, and his sharp, dark eyes are suddenly tired. He drains his schnapps and serves himself and* ABEL*)*

HOLLINGER   In fear there's a hellish fury. Everyone's afraid now, afraid to the point of madness. All the meek, little officials and their good-natured wives, all the soldiers loafing about the barracks and wishing they were back at the war, all the poor farmers who get nothing for their produce, all the teachers who no longer believe in what their textbooks say—they're all afraid, and soon their fear will turn to fury. Do you want to see that day, my dear Abel? No, you don't. If you're not already battered to death, you'd rather perform your circus stunts at the South Pole than here in Berlin *when the meek rise up and their fear turns to fury.*

(As HOLLINGER *bares his long, yellow teeth, his bad breath reaches* ABEL*'s face. He opens his jacket to reveal a pistol that he keeps in a pocket on the outside of his vest, just by the left armpit)*

HOLLINGER   No one's going to take me alive, anyway, and cut off my cock. You can be sure of that, my dear Abel. Here's to you, my boy, my clever little acrobat. We'll make out all right, you'll see. A circus always gets by. Trust Papa Hollinger! Why don't you say something, my dear Abel?

ABEL I'm listening. What you say is interesting. But frankly, I couldn't care less. I swing on my trapeze, I eat, sleep, and fuck. What the hell am I to say? I don't believe all that political bunkum. The Jews are as stupid as everyone else. If a Jew gets into trouble, it's his own fault. He gets into trouble because he's stupid. I'm not going to be stupid, even if I am a Jew. So I won't get into trouble. Now you know, Papa Hollinger. Thanks for the dinner and the money. I must go. I'm meeting Manuela at four.

4

At the cabaret Zum Blauen Esel, the Sunday afternoon show is in progress. The hall, which was originally a garage, extends like a crooked bowel far into the building. A few spectators, mostly elderly men, are sitting at the tightly packed tables. Three waitresses are hanging about at the bar, which has been set up in a narrow doorway. They are chatting and smoking. A small band, squashed into the orchestra pit, is making quite a din despite its modest size. On the stage, which looks more like a cupboard stuck onto the end wall, stands a young woman who is trying to make herself heard above the music. She is singing a song about a girl who has some candy, and it's just fine and dandy; she's so kind that if you've a mind, she'll let you suck her candy. The girl accompanies these words by rather clumsy, mistimed gestures. She is tall and thin and wears an ill-fitting dress with a bustle. A carelessly fixed blue wig is perched on her head.

ABEL, *who is not yet sober, weaves his way to the bar, greets the waitresses, has a glass of beer put into his hand, then sinks heavily onto the nearest chair. The place is dank and chilly, and smells of cabbage soup and dead mice.*

As the girl, with a movement that has no pretense to grace, lets the last covering fall, she exposes a thin but well-shaped body with broad shoulders and high, round breasts. The music ends in tumult, and the purple silk curtain with its obscene designs is closed with a violent jerk.

Someone applauds; otherwise there is a dead silence. The members of the band sit for a few moments as though paralyzed, worn out by previous efforts. ABEL *gets up and heads toward a narrow door at the side of the stage. At that moment the band takes heart and starts to blare out a march. The curtain is jerked open, and in march four girls in guards' uniforms, with bare bottoms and shiny helmets with plumes. Stumping to and fro on the stage in black, high-heeled bootees, they sing, or rather shout, about the old guard who never gives in through thick and thin.*

ABEL *goes down a few steps; stoops under some dripping pipes; knocks at an unpainted wooden door; and enters a cramped, partitioned-off space that has been furnished with a wooden table fixed to the wall and covered with a torn oilcloth, a cracked mirror, two rickety chairs, a sink, a jug, and a bucket full of yellowish slop. The unpainted boarded partition is adorned with cuttings from magazines.*

The girl who has just sung has wrapped herself in a stained makeup robe, a thick-knitted cardigan, and a large shawl. She is putting on a pair of heavy woolen stockings when she catches sight of ABEL. *Her face lights up but darkens immediately.*

MANUELA   What's wrong?

ABEL   When I got home last night, Max had blown his brains out.

(MANUELA *sits down on one of the chairs. Her face is blank. Slowly she takes off the blue wig, runs her fingers through her shingled, auburn hair, and smoothes the bangs with her palm. It is force of habit*)

MANUELA   I knew he'd do it.

ABEL   I tried to keep an eye on him, but I never really thought he would. Not Max.

(*They sit there distressed and at a loss. The girl rubs a spot on the oilcloth with her forefinger.* ABEL *takes out a pack of cigarettes and offers her one; when she declines, he returns the pack to his pocket*)

MANUELA   He had some sort of job the last few weeks. Have you any idea what it was?

ABEL   I asked him several times, but he only said the pay was good and told me to mind my own business. He left a letter for you.

(ABEL *hands her a crumpled envelope containing a few dollar bills and a sheet of paper covered with Max's illegible scribble*)

MANUELA   It's almost impossible to read his writing. No, I can't. Can you?

(*She hands the letter to* ABEL, *who sits down on the other chair. He sits for a long time in silence, trying to make out his brother's message*)

ABEL   No, I can't make it out. (*Pause*) Yes, now I see, mixed up here with all the rest: "Someone said to me the other day that man is a misconstruction. I asked him to prove his assertion. All he said was, 'Look about

you, there's your proof.' I did as he said. I looked about me but didn't think . . ." *(Stops reading)* I can't read this . . . Yes, here's something: "Poisoning is going on all the time . . ."

(ABEL *looks up and meets* MANUELA'*s eyes. She shakes her head*)

MANUELA *(Repeating)* "Poisoning is going on all the time . . ."

ABEL I didn't see much of him these last weeks.

MANUELA But you lived in the same room?

ABEL   He was hardly ever at home. One morning we came to blows. *(Pause)* I had brought a whore back. She was still there when he came home early in the morning. He wanted her himself for a while. She agreed, though he paid only half-price. Then he started quarreling and got rough with her. At last I had to give him a thrashing. Then he began to scream like a small child. I didn't hit him very hard. I had to think of his bad wrist.

MANUELA *(Interrupting)*   Christ, I must change for the finale! Can you help me?

*(*MANUELA *sheds her shawl, cardigan, makeup robe, and stockings; unhooks a creation curiously like a swimming costume; and slips into it.* ABEL *helps her with the buttons and a belt with a dark-yellow bow)*

ABEL   I didn't know you performed.

MANUELA   I didn't. But one of the girls got the flu, and I suggested I take her place and do her number. The boss thought it was a good idea, so now I'm a cabaret singer and get thirty-five million a day. It's not enough to live on, but it's something.

ABEL   Do you go with men?

MANUELA *(Rushed)*   Can't you call for me this evening and we'll go somewhere for supper? Take charge of Max's money for the time being. There's nowhere to hide it here.

(She kisses him on the cheek and slips out. ABEL *remains standing for a few moments. He hears the regular thump of the finale and all the feet stamping on the wooden floor:*

"Berlin, Berlin, Berlinerin. Berlin, Berlin mit leich-
tem Sinn."

*When he opens the door, he sees a man standing in the gloom
of the passage. He is an angular man with a sallow, lean face
and thin, gray hair above a high brow. His eyes are clear and
calm behind a pair of thick glasses. He stands propped against
the wooden wall, looking at the lighted stage. He turns toward* ABEL *and smiles politely)*

HANS　Funny seeing everything from the side like this.
(Pause) I seem to recognize you. Didn't we meet years
ago? Perhaps we smoked our first cigarette together?

(ABEL *shakes his head)*

HANS　No? But if I say Amalfi, a summer's day twenty-
six years ago? Our parents had summer cottages next
door to each other. You had an elder sister named, let
me see . . . Rebecka! Well?

ABEL　*(Shaking his head)*　Would you mind letting me
pass? I'm in rather a hurry.

HANS　*(Smiling)* Why, of course. *(Pause)* Abel Rosenberg.

(ABEL *turns at the door and shakes his head, but he knows he's
been recognized and blushes. He therefore bows stiffly and slips
out through the narrow and cluttered emergency exit)*

5

It is dark and even colder than it had been in the afternoon. The mist has turned to an icy drizzle, and the deserted sidewalks shine blackly in the dim street lighting.

ABEL *walks at a fast pace to keep warm. He is about to turn into a side street when he stops at the sight of a small group of people on the sidewalk. He first sees five boys in Neues Vaterland uniforms. Around them stand a few bewildered civilians, and farther down the street two policemen are stationed with their backs to the crowd.*

ABEL *gets closer. He now sees that a tall man in a black overcoat, hat, and a pair of gold-rimmed glasses is arguing with one of the uniformed boys. A well-dressed elderly woman, possibly the man's mother, tugs at his sleeve and tries to quiet him. The man is talking very loudly and quickly, and* ABEL *can't understand what he is saying. Suddenly one of the boys hits him in the face, knocking off his hat and glasses. The clatter of a bucket is heard, and the woman has a scouring cloth thrust into her hand, the man a scrubbing brush. They kneel down. Under the supervision of the five young men, they begin to scrub the sidewalk.*

One of the boys pokes a dog turd up out of the gutter. He says something to the kneeling man, who slowly bends forward. For a moment it looks as if he is going to touch the excrement with his lips, then he shakes his head and shouts something to the policemen, who have begun to walk away.

Then the beating begins. The spectators vanish like flickering shadows, and ABEL, *too, hurries away.*

For a long time he can hear the woman's screams and the dull thud of the truncheons on the cowering bodies.

A small bar comes into sight a few steps below the street level. ABEL tumbles in and for some moments stands confused in the almost empty room. Recollecting the envelope with Max's money, he peels a one-dollar bill from the wad and lays it on the counter.

6

In an old-fashioned, middle-class apartment on Hölderlinstrasse
MANUELA *rents a large room which is so cluttered with late-Victorian paraphernalia that it seems cramped despite the space.*
ABEL *has sunk into an armchair fitted with an antimacassar.*
He is very drunk.

MANUELA   I don't want you to go to the boardinghouse tonight. You can sleep here with me. Stand up so that I can take your coat off. I'll make some real tea, nice and hot. It will do you good.

(MANUELA *gets him out of the chair, pulls off his coat, and lets it fall to the floor. He throws his arms around her waist and leans his head on her shoulder.* MANUELA *pats him on the back, staggering under the weight. He is shaken by violent, tearless sobbing)*

7

The same night—the night before Monday, November 5—a woman's body is found at the water's edge at Treptow and taken to the Institute of Forensic Medicine at police headquarters on

Alexanderplatz. The most horrifying thing is that her genitals have been lacerated, possibly by a broken bottle, and the body shows other signs of assault. Two ribs are broken, but the face is uninjured—a round, childish, rather ravaged face with no makeup and a broad brow. The long hair is done up on top. A preliminary examination shows that the woman was drowned in the shallow water. She was wearing a heavy winter coat, but under the coat she was naked. No identification papers are found, only an engagement ring, on which is engraved, "Max/ July 1923."

8

At four o'clock in the morning, ABEL *is awakened by the opening of the hall door in the passage outside* MANUELA*'s room. He listens in sudden fear: heavy footsteps approach, stop; another door is opened; there is a strange, dull noise; something is lifted; something is put down with a thud.*

MANUELA *(Sleepily)*   It's only the man changing the cans in the privy. He comes every Monday morning about four.

ABEL   Dear God!

(He sits leaning against the wall, listening to the receding noise: the hall door being shut, the echo of footsteps on the curving staircase, the men talking in the quiet street, the clip-clop of horses' hooves, the cartwheels on the cobblestones)

ABEL   We used to spend the summer at Amalfi for
Mama's sake. She had weak lungs. Papa was ambassa-
dor in Copenhagen in those days. I remember Max and
I used to play with a boy called Hans Vergérus. The
family was from Düsseldorf—the father was some big-
wig supreme court judge or something of the kind.
The families were on visiting terms, and we children
used to play together. Hans fell in love with my sister.
I think they were even secretly engaged. Mama didn't
like Hans. Come to think of it, no one did. But everyone considered him a genius. Once we caught a cat and
tied it down. Hans cut it open—it was still alive—and
showed me how its heart beat, fast, fast. Then he
poked one of its eyes out with a sharp, little knife and
showed me how the pupil continued to react.

   I told Rebecka what we'd done. She went right to
Hans and asked him if it was true. He said it was a lie,
that it was a dead cat, and that I was making it all up.
The funny thing was, I almost believed I *had* made it
up, mostly to please Hans. So we went on being
friends. Then Mama died and Papa was transferred.
Ten years ago I ran across Hans in Heidelberg, when
we were there with the circus.

MANUELA   Yes, I remember.

ABEL   You don't at all. You weren't there.

MANUELA   I do remember meeting Hans! Max intro-
duced us. He was in a hurry, he had a lecture—he was
a professor at the university. I remember exactly, and
the way Max laughed and said, "He *was* in a hurry all
of a sudden. Do you think he didn't want to know us?"

ABEL   No, no . . . As *I* recall it, he was pleased to see us,
although he was in a hurry. I think he even wanted to

take us to dinner, but we had to refuse because of our performances.

MANUELA *(Yawning)* You're wrong, but it doesn't matter.

ABEL I met him yesterday.

MANUELA Hans?

ABEL Didn't you see him? He was at the cabaret.

MANUELA No.

ABEL Are you sure?

MANUELA If I'd seen him I'd say so, wouldn't I?

(ABEL *lies down, wide awake.*

A car is heard down in the street, then another, and another. There is a singing in the waterpipes. Someone has awakened in the apartment above and is walking across the creaking parquet floor. The street lamp, which has been swaying in the wind and illuminating the room with its restless, flickering glow, suddenly goes out and a faint light can be seen at the edge of the painted blind. A newspaper is pushed through the letter slot and thuds onto the hall floor.

The city of Berlin prepares for the new day, Monday, November 5. This shabby, poverty-stricken city is inhabited by countless people who are waking up to new hopelessness, new dread, new attempts at survival.

A factory whistle cuts through the iron-gray dawn. The first trolley car of the day clatters down the endless street; wheels and rails screech as it turns out of Hölderlinstrasse onto the big avenue.

ABEL *goes to the window and draws the blind back a bit.*

He stands looking down at the street and at the windows in
the big stone building opposite, where lights are being turned
on and people are moving through the rooms. A milk cart, its
driver slouched over the load, half asleep, is drawn by a lean
horse and rattles down the street)

9

An hour later the alarm clock rings. ABEL *has fallen asleep in*
an armchair. He has dropped a lighted cigarette on the carpet,
and it has burned a hole before going out. MANUELA *is standing*
behind a screen, making coffee on a spirit stove.

MANUELA   The advantage of meeting influential people is that you can have real coffee for breakfast. I've got the fire going nicely, but it takes a while before it gets hot. I've filled the jug in the niche of the tiled stove. The water will be warm by the time you want to wash.

ABEL   Do you get firewood in the same way?

MANUELA   I do know a wood dealer, as a matter of fact. But I don't know anyone who can give me butter, so you'll have to make do with this jam, which is no doubt mostly chemicals.

ABEL   I owe you a dollar. We must make a note of it.

MANUELA   Never mind.

ABEL   You'd better take charge of the money before it all goes on booze.

MANUELA   Do you drink much?

ABEL   When I have money.

MANUELA   *(Astonished)*   So you don't want to go back to the circus?

ABEL   What's the use, without Max?

MANUELA   We must get a new partner, of course.

ABEL   You know as well as I do it's impossible.

MANUELA   I know nothing of the sort. *(Pause)* Well, then, we must think up a new number with just you and me. What about something with dogs? A comic trapeze

number with us and four dachshunds dressed up.
While we hang upside down on the trapezes, swinging
backward and forward, the dogs fly between us with
their ears flapping.

ABEL   Very funny.

MANUELA   There are thousands of things to do if you
really wanted to. We could think up a conjuring act!
I know a marvelous magician who's retired now—
Markus, you know. He lives at Lichterfelde. We could
take over his show.

ABEL   I don't know. But this business with Max has . . .

*(His voice trails off. He looks down at his hand, which is
crumbling a slice of bread. Time and again he tries to say
something but merely shakes his head. His eyes blink; the lids
grow red)*

MANUELA   Ever since I met Max, you've been my big
brother. You and I must stick together now.

ABEL   *(Groping for words)*   It's like waking up from a
nightmare and finding that reality is worse than the
dream.

MANUELA   *(In surprise)*   But Abel, my dear, we're all
right! We have everything we need.

ABEL   I can't make out what it is. Last night I saw them
beating up a man. The police just turned their backs.

MANUELA   Abel dear, listen to me, please. You're awfully tired and have been drinking too much lately. I'm
going to take care of you now and in a few days you'll

be much better, you'll see. We'll talk things over, but just now I must hurry or I'll be late for work.

ABEL *(Amazed)* Work?

MANUELA I've an extra job.

ABEL At this time of the morning?

MANUELA Yes. At this very time of the morning. And I mustn't be late.

ABEL What sort of job is it?

MANUELA I don't know exactly. It's secret, anyway.

ABEL Secret?

MANUELA I was only joking. I work at an office. Sticking on stamps and running errands.

ABEL What sort of office?

MANUELA Something to do with import and export. I really don't know.

ABEL What's the name of the firm?

MANUELA What the devil is it now . . . Ferkel's the name. Ferkel und Sohn.

ABEL Where's the office?

MANUELA On Bayerstrasse. It's a small side street up by the abattoirs. You're going on like a jealous husband.

(MANUELA *laughs and pats him on the cheek. She gets up from the table and begins to clear the dishes*)

MANUELA　You're your brother's brother, and no mistake. Max was always at me like that.

ABEL　No, let me wash up and tidy the room, then at least I'll have something to do. You get ready, as you're in a hurry.

MANUELA　I'll be back about two, then we can have dinner. Try to get hold of some meat, now that we have some money.

ABEL　Forty-nine dollars.

MANUELA　Heavens, a fortune!

(*She washes and dresses quickly, pulls the cloche hat down over her auburn hair, swings her coat over her shoulders, hunts for her purse, buttons up the straps of her shoes, checks that the seams of her stockings are straight, and puts on lipstick—all in a tearing rush*)

MANUELA　My trolley's coming! I'll just catch it if I dash. We'll make out, you see if we don't.

(*And she is gone.* ABEL *stands with the wad of bills in his hand, then he begins to walk around the room. He stops in front of a large desk by one of the three windows. Slowly and methodically he hunts through drawer after drawer. It doesn't take him long. In a metal box hidden behind a lot of junk he finds a small wad of dollar bills.*

ABEL *dresses quickly and puts on the old summer overcoat, which has lost yet another button. He tiptoes through the long passage; glimpses a large kitchen, where two girls are having breakfast; turns a corner; finds the hall door; and is about to open it quietly when a faint voice calls him by name)*

VOICE   Herr Rosenberg!

ABEL   Yes?

VOICE   Would you mind coming in here for a moment?

(Leading off the hall is a half-open door; a sunbeam falls across the carpet and the scratched parquet. He opens the door cautiously and steps into a large room with a bay window and vaulted ceiling with graceful plaster ornaments. By the wall is a richly decorated double bed. This room too is crammed with old-fashioned furniture, pictures, and bric-a-brac. Despite the strong sunlight, the room is in semi-darkness, as the heavy curtains are only partly opened.

ABEL discovers a little old lady almost hidden behind a high-backed armchair. She detaches herself slowly from the shadows and comes forward. She is wearing a long dressing gown of old-fashioned cut, the iron-gray hair is screwed up in a knob on top of her head, the face is round and very smooth, almost rosy, and the gray eyes are magnified by thick glasses. A crooked back and a hump by the right shoulder deform the thin body)

FRAU HOLLE   My name is Frau Holle. I am Manuela's landlady.

(She puts out a slender, well-shaped hand. It is dry but cold. ABEL bows)

FRAU HOLLE   Manuela just had time to tell me about you on her way out. You are welcome to stay here with me for a short time. Manuela's roommate has gone to Italy for a couple of weeks. Excuse me if I lie down on the

bed. These sudden changes in the weather make my
back ache. All the same, it's nice with a peep of sun in
November, is it not, Herr Rosenberg?

*(After having arranged a mound of pillows behind her aching
back,* FRAU HOLLE *settles down on her big bed and throws a
rug over her legs)*

FRAU HOLLE   Would you care for a glass of sherry? You
can get it yourself from the cupboard over there. No,
not that one, the other cupboard. Yes, there. Do you
see that little crystal decanter to the right? That's the
one. Bring two glasses. I think I'll have a drop, too.
Thank you, Herr Rosenberg. *Prosit!*

(They drink to each other. FRAU HOLLE *holds the beautifully shaped glass up to the light)*

FRAU HOLLE   I am very attached to Manuela. Being her brother-in-law, you know her better than I do, of course, but I must say that Manuela is a very unusual young person. If you'll forgive my saying so, I'm as fond of her as if she were my own daughter.

(The gray eyes behind the glasses are turned toward ABEL, *and he sees an expression of fear in the pale face)*

FRAU HOLLE   She's so kind and naïve. It's as if all the terrible things going on around us didn't concern her. *(Pause)* I think your sister-in-law is heading for trouble, Herr Rosenberg.

ABEL   I haven't noticed anything.

FRAU HOLLE   The odd thing about Manuela is that she doesn't defend herself, if you know what I mean. *(Pause)* Nothing must happen to her.

ABEL   I'll keep an eye on her as best I can.

FRAU HOLLE   Take this new work now. There's something odd about it. The Society for Church Democracy, what is that, Herr Rosenberg? It isn't even in the phone book. *(Pause)* I know that she and her friend gadded about with men for a time. I almost thought it was better. Now I don't know what she's up to. And it worries me.

ABEL   I must go now, Frau Holle. By the way, what is the rent? Maybe you'd like to be paid in advance?

FRAU HOLLE   It doesn't matter, but if you have money, I
don't mind. I'm a poor widow. The pension from my
husband doesn't go far. You have dollars, haven't you?
Shall we say ten dollars a month? Or is that too much?

ABEL   I'll put the money here on the tray. Is that all
right?

*(He has taken out a ten-dollar bill and slips it under the
empty wineglass. Then he gets up to go, but the old lady checks
him with a gesture)*

FRAU HOLLE   Have you been crying?

ABEL   No. Why?

FRAU HOLLE   It just looked as if you had. Forgive me.

ABEL   Good-bye, Frau Holle.

FRAU HOLLE   Do come in for a chat some time. I can't get
about much with this pain. I can't even go to concerts
at the old Opera House, though it's not far away.
Good-bye, Herr Rosenberg, and take care of your sister-in-law.

*(*ABEL *bows again and makes his escape. Down in the street
he runs for the trolley car and jumps on, clinging to the
outside of the overloaded rear platform)*

10

FRAU HEMSE *is at the little reception desk busy with accounts.*
The moment she catches sight of ABEL *she bustles up to him.*

FRAU HEMSE   The police are waiting up there in your
room. They won't even let us clean up after the terrible—

(ABEL *murmurs something soothing to* FRAU HEMSE, *who is*
very overwrought, and runs upstairs. The door of the room
is open. INSPECTOR BAUER *is standing in the middle of the*
floor; the cigar in his mouth has gone out. A plainclothes
policeman is lounging by the window)

BAUER   Good morning, Herr Rosenberg. We've been
waiting for you. May I ask where you've been all
night?

ABEL   I could hardly sleep in this room.

BAUER   I realize that. But you could have told Frau
Hemse where you were going. Where have you been?

ABEL   With my sister-in-law.

BAUER   She lives at Thirty-five Hölderlinstrasse, doesn't
she?

ABEL   Yes, I think so.

BAUER   Think?

ABEL *(Nervous)*   I think it's Number Thirty-five.

BAUER   Well, now you know.

ABEL   May I pack a few belongings?

BAUER   I'm sorry. Not yet.

ABEL   Oh.

(Sits down)

BAUER   I must ask you to come with us to the morgue.
It's a matter of identifying a girl.

ABEL *(Frightened)*   Is it necessary?

BAUER *(Formally)*   I'm afraid I must insist.

ABEL   Well, we'd better get going.

*(At the morgue, two younger men in stained white coats
accompany them several floors down in a wide elevator with
an exit on two sides. BAUER relights his cigar. His silent
colleague looks in his case and finds a stump, which he also
lights. The inspector offers ABEL a cigarette. ABEL declines)*

BAUER   I'd advise you to smoke in there. It helps.

*(The elevator has now reached the bottom. They get out and
walk down a long passage painted green and lighted by sickly-
yellow lamps. The smell of Formalin and the stench of decay-*

*ing bodies get stronger. One of the white-coated men unlocks
a wide, iron door on which is a letter and a figure. They enter
a very large tiled room illuminated by several bright lights.
In the middle of the floor stand a number of long, wooden
tables with grooves at the edges. Along the walls are wheeled
stretchers. On each stretcher lies a body covered with a dirty
sheet. The two men unfold a typed piece of paper, which they
study in silence. Then one of them goes up to a stretcher, checks
the figures on the label attached to the ankle of the deceased,
pulls the stretcher to the middle of the floor, and uncovers the
naked body)*

BAUER　Do you recognize that girl?

ABEL　Yes.

BAUER　Who is she?

ABEL　Grethe Hofer.

BAUER　In what way do you know her?

ABEL　She was engaged to my brother.

BAUER　When did you see her last?

ABEL　A week ago.

BAUER　Was your brother on good terms with—

ABEL　Yes, I think so.

BAUER　Fräulein Hofer has been assaulted. Also, her
genitals have been mutilated with a sharp object, probably a broken bottle. Cause of death: drowning.

(BAUER *signals to the men to cover the body. When this is done, they wheel the stretcher back to its place by the wall but at once pull out another stretcher. The sheet is removed, exposing a man's body in the first stages of decay*)

BAUER   Do you recognize this man?

ABEL *(With an effort)*   No, I don't.

BAUER   Are you quite sure?

ABEL   No.

BAUER   Think hard, Herr Rosenberg. It's important.

ABEL   He's like someone.

BAUER   Who?

ABEL *(Helplessly)*   He's like my father.

BAUER   You can do better than that.

ABEL   That's all I can think of. He's like my father, who died five years ago.

BAUER   This man has been killed by someone sticking a very thin hypodermic needle into his heart. Then a liquid of some sort has been injected into the left ventricle—a poison that must have caused the victim hideous pain before death, which probably didn't occur until several hours later. So you haven't seen this man before?

(ABEL *shakes his head*)

BAUER *(To the men)*   Take him away, please.

(The two men cover the body and wheel it away, but immediately they bring another stretcher, which they uncover. The deceased is a middle-aged woman with a bitter face and an emaciated body)

BAUER   Have you seen this woman before?

ABEL   Yes.

BAUER   Who is she?

ABEL   I don't know. But I've seen her.

BAUER   Where have you seen her?

ABEL *(In distress)*   I think she delivered papers. I used to meet her at Frau Hemse's boardinghouse. Once she helped me up to my room when I was too drunk to manage on my own.

BAUER   Her name was Maria Stern.

ABEL   I didn't know that.

BAUER   She hanged herself in the basement room, where she lived with her husband and two children. But she left a very strange letter, hard to make out and totally muddled. She said she had been frightened to death and that the pain was unbearable.

(ABEL stares at BAUER, who returns his look calmly, now and then puffing at his cigar)

ABEL   I don't think I can stand this.

BAUER   Just a little longer, if you don't mind.

(MARIA STERN *has already been wheeled away and another body brought forward. It is that of a boy about sixteen. The chest is crushed and the throat cut right to the vertebral column. The dark eyes are staring, the black curly hair is matted with blood, and the forehead is shattered*)

BAUER   Have you ever seen this boy?

ABEL   No.

BAUER   He did the lighting at Zum Blauen Esel. Did you ever see him there?

ABEL   No.

BAUER   Odd.

ABEL   I've only been there once or twice.

BAUER   He used to stand just by the entrance, in charge of a movable spotlight that was trained on the artists. You must have seen him.

ABEL   Yes. *(Whispering)* It's possible.

BAUER   His name was Josef Birnbaum.

(ABEL *makes no reply*)

BAUER   We're not certain how he was killed. He seems to have been run over by a heavy truck, but something tells us that before that he was assaulted or tortured.

ABEL   Why are you showing me all this?

BAUER   During the last month seven mysterious deaths have occurred. In your vicinity, Herr Rosenberg.

ABEL   But surely you don't suspect me?

BAUER   Come along to my office, and I'll give you a pick-me-up.

11

BAUER *unlocks the door of his office, a cramped, shabby room with a few sticks of furniture and grubby curtains. The window looks out onto a narrow yard, on the other side of which is a row of barred windows. The inspector takes off his overcoat and jacket, and puts on an alpaca jacket with patches on the elbows. The taciturn plainclothes policeman has sat down on a chair by the door.*

BAUER   Sit down, Rosenberg. Would you like some coffee? Well, it can hardly be called coffee, but it's something.

(He shouts through the door for someone to bring three cups of coffee and some rusks, if there are any. He sits down at the desk, gets up again, and sits on a chair opposite ABEL *so that he is almost touching him.* FRÄULEIN DORST *comes in carrying a small tray, on which she is balancing three cups of black liquid and a yellow metal basket with square rusks. She asks quietly if she is to stay or to wait outside.* BAUER *tells her to wait, he'll call her if he needs her. As she is going out he asks if Inspector Lohmann has left a message. He hasn't)*

BAUER   Drink your coffee, Rosenberg.

(ABEL *obeys in silence*)

BAUER   Christ, it's hot in here! One day it's freezing and the next you can fry eggs on the walls.

(ABEL *says nothing*)

BAUER   Not very chatty, are you, Rosenberg?

(ABEL *shrugs*)

BAUER   Can you account for your movements on the evening of Sunday, October twenty-eighth?

(ABEL *shakes his head*)

BAUER   Oh, you can't.

ABEL   I was drunk. If you ask me about Friday, October nineteenth, for instance, I was drunk then, too. I've been drunk every night since we left the circus. Sometimes I've been drunk in the mornings, too; sometimes not until two o'clock; but always at night. I've no recollection of what happened to me in the evenings. It's like a lot of blurred snapshots.

BAUER   Snapshots of what?

ABEL   Whores, mostly. Naked and hard at it. You want to know how I could afford both whores and drink? Well, I'd saved a bit of money. We were pretty well paid, being a well-known troupe.

BAUER   There's something that doesn't add up.

(ABEL *is silent*)

BAUER   If you were a well-known troupe with a good income and a good reputation, why did you start drinking after you left the circus?

(ABEL *is silent*)

BAUER   I'd be grateful if you answered my question.

ABEL   I'm an alcoholic.

(ABEL *gives a forced smile*)

BAUER   A famous trapeze artist who's an alcoholic? Don't try to kid me.

ABEL   Maybe I didn't feel welcome in your beautiful city.

(BAUER *sits down behind his desk, hunts among papers and files, finds what he is looking for, and begins scratching away with a sharply pointed pen. A long silence.* ABEL *grows afraid and starts pacing to and fro*)

BAUER   Sit down, Rosenberg.

ABEL   *(Sitting down)*   Why do I have to be here?

BAUER   I thought you might be able to help me with seven unsolved deaths.

ABEL   How could I?

BAUER   Oh, who knows?

ABEL   But what's the use?

BAUER   What do you mean, Rosenberg?

ABEL   Tomorrow the abyss will open and everything
will vanish in a final catastrophe. So why bother about
a few paltry deaths?

BAUER   I'll tell you, Rosenberg. I'm doing it for my own
sake. I know as well as you do that the catastrophe may
be upon us within a few hours. People are starving.
I'm told that the rate of exchange for the dollar is five
billion marks. The French have occupied the Ruhr.
We've just paid a billion in gold to the victors. At every
damned place of work there are bolshevik agitators. In
Munich a Herr Hitler is preparing a *Putsch* with thousands of starving soldiers and uniformed madmen. We
have a government that doesn't know which way to
turn from one day to the next. Tomorrow or maybe
the day after, disaster will strike and we'll be drowned
in blood, if we haven't already been burned to death.
Everyone's afraid. So am I—I can't sleep at night for
fear. Nothing works properly except fear. On Friday
I wanted to go to Stettin to see my old mother, who'll
be eighty, but *there wasn't a timetable any more.* There
was a train that *might* go, but no timetable. Imagine a
Germany without timetables, Rosenberg. So what
does Inspector Bauer do in the midst of his own fear
and other people's horror? What does one do in a
nightmare that happens to be real? Inspector Bauer
attends to his work. He tries to create a little patch of
order and reason in the midst of a chaos of hopeless
dissolution. And he's not alone, Rosenberg. All over
Germany millions and millions of petty officials, just
as terrified and just as insignificant, are thinking in
exactly the same way. We pretend from hour to hour

that the world is normal. At a quarter to eight in the morning, we sit on our backsides dictating a meaningless letter to some Fräulein Dorst, who knows that the letter is meaningless and that no one's going to read it and that both she and the letter will probably go up in flames before it's even typed out in five copies, according to regulations. You get drunk every day. That's also respectable, Rosenberg, though I'd be happier if you swung about on your trapeze with your colleagues —in that way you'd fight your fear much more effectively. So now you know why I sit here investigating something which I think is extremely odd, not to say horrible. And now I must ask you to keep quiet for a few minutes while I write a few lines to Inspector Lohmann, who's working on another case that also seems insane. We'll go on with our talk in a minute, Rosenberg. I won't be long.

ABEL   What do you suspect me of?

(BAUER *goes on writing with his scratchy pen*)

ABEL   Aren't I entitled to a lawyer?

BAUER *(Writing)*   This is a talk, not an interrogation.

ABEL   You're taking it out on me.

(BAUER *writes*)

ABEL   You're trying to frighten me.

(BAUER *writes*)

ABEL   Answer, for Christ's sake!

BAUER   Drink your coffee and shut up.

(ABEL's *anguish mounts. He lifts his coffee cup but slams it down again. He hunts in his coat for a cigarette but can't find one*)

ABEL   I need a cigarette.

(BAUER *writes*)

ABEL   I know why you're trying to frighten me. You're getting at me because I'm a Jew.

(BAUER *looks up, smiles, goes on scratching.*
  Suddenly ABEL *begins to scream. It happens very suddenly. He yells at the top of his voice, is silent for a few moments, and covers his face with his hands. Another scream forces its way out between his lips, then he makes a rush for the door. The plainclothes constable stops him and flings him against the wall.* BAUER *goes up to him but is struck in the face and falls against a chair.* ABEL *dashes for the door again, knocks the policeman down, and gets the door open. In the outer office there is tumult:* FRÄULEIN DORST *lets out a scream; three policemen leap up from their desks;* ABEL *jumps over a counter and runs down a passage, only to be stopped by an iron-barred gate. The pursuers catch up with him, and someone hits him on the head with a truncheon. He fights like a maniac. After another blow on the head he slumps down in a daze, uttering despairing and inarticulate cries. A third blow silences him and he grows heavy and limp. They lay him flat on the floor, turn him over face down, and bind his hands and feet.*
  When he comes to he is lying on a wooden bunk in a cell with bars all along one wall. He sits up but begins to retch. He has a splitting headache and loses his balance as he tries to stumble over to the waterpipe. He manages to turn on the faucet. The pipe hisses and gurgles, but no water comes out.

A constable is standing on the other side of the bars, watching him impassively. ABEL *tries to tell him that he needs water. The constable says something in German and shakes his head.* ABEL *tries again, but his throat is swollen after all the screaming and he can only whisper. The constable shakes his head and leaves him)*

12

Late in the afternoon the cell door is opened and the constable tells ABEL *in German that he has a visitor. As* ABEL *doesn't understand, the man indicates that he is to go with him.*

They enter a square room with a barred window high up in the wall. In the middle of the room is a wooden table with a chair on either side.

MANUELA *is there. She jumps to her feet and goes toward* ABEL, *but the constable motions her to sit down again. A policewoman is sitting on the right behind the door.*

POLICEWOMAN   I'm here because I speak English. If you say or do anything improper, I must put an end to the visit immediately, and Herr Rosenberg will be taken back to his cell. You are allowed to smoke. You have ten minutes.

MANUELA   You're all bruised.

ABEL   Never mind.

MANUELA   I've spoken to Inspector Bauer. He was very kind and understanding.

ABEL   Oh.

MANUELA   He said he wanted to help you.

(ABEL *looks at her*)

MANUELA   He said you started shouting and fighting. He said you went on as if you'd gone crazy.

ABEL   What's wrong, Manuela?

MANUELA   With me?

ABEL   You look funny.

MANUELA   Do I? In what way?

ABEL   You look as if you had a temperature.

MANUELA   Do I?

(*She takes out a small mirror and looks at herself carefully. Then she laughs and pats her hair*)

ABEL   Your eyes have a funny look.

MANUELA   I'm just worried.

ABEL   Why?

MANUELA   My savings have been stolen.

ABEL   Have they?

MANUELA   I suppose you don't know where they've gone?

ABEL   I didn't know you had any savings.

MANUELA   They've gone, anyway.

ABEL   Lucky I'm in charge of Max's money.

MANUELA   That's just it.

ABEL   What?

MANUELA   Inspector Bauer said they had found Max's money when they searched you. It's illegal to have dollars, did you know?

ABEL   No.

MANUELA   Bauer asked me if I knew where Max had gotten hold of that money.

ABEL   Well?

MANUELA   I said they were our savings. We'd been in Switzerland with the circus and several of the artists had cashed their salaries into dollars before the German tour. No one knew it was illegal.

ABEL   Who do you think has stolen your money?

MANUELA   What did you say?

ABEL   Manuela!

MANUELA   Yes?

ABEL   You're not listening.

MANUELA   Just a moment.

(She sits with her eyes closed. Forehead and cheeks are flushed as with fever, and small beads of perspiration have broken out on her upper lip)

ABEL   You're ill. *(To the policewoman)* She's ill.

(The policewoman gets up and goes over to MANUELA. *She tells the constable to fetch a glass of water and keeps asking* MANUELA *if she feels ill, if she'd like to lie down.* MANUELA *shakes her head, her eyes closed.*
   The constable returns with a tin mug of water. MANUELA *sips it. Slowly the nausea passes and she opens her eyes. For a moment it seems as if she doesn't quite know where she is. But her head clears quickly, and she smiles apologetically)*

MANUELA   Thank you, I'm all right. I feel much better. It's just that I haven't eaten all day, and I've been worried.

(She lays her palms on the table and gravely looks at her hands for a long time)

POLICEWOMAN   I'd like to point out that you have only two minutes left.

ABEL   Manuela?

MANUELA   Yes, Herr Rosenberg?

ABEL   What have you been doing today?

MANUELA   I was at the office, then I went home to have dinner with you. I'd come by a piece of meat from a butcher I know. While I was waiting for you, Bauer turned up and sat there for at least half an hour. Then I had to go down to the cabaret to return a dress I'd borrowed from Else. Then I took a trolley car and came here to you.

ABEL   That office . . .

MANUELA   Yes, what about it?

ABEL   Is it export and import, or is it something to do with the church? Or is it neither?

MANUELA   I work at a brothel in the mornings. It's not forbidden, as far as I know. It's a damned respectable brothel, let me tell you. Only diplomats and managing directors and famous actors go there, so it's a classy place, if you must know. *(Miserably)* Idiot.

(The door opens and INSPECTOR BAUER *comes in. He greets* MANUELA *politely, nods to* ABEL, *sits down at the table, clasps his hands, and sits for a moment in silence)*

BAUER   I'm going to let you out, Herr Rosenberg. In spite of the way you attacked me and my colleagues. My God, the way you let fly! But then you're a circus artist. *(Pause)* As I said, I'm going to let you go, and you needn't worry about any unpleasant consequences. We've talked the matter over and are of the opinion that your nerves are to blame for the rumpus. So much for that.

*(*BAUER *clears his throat and looks up at the window. It is now dark outside. Then he looks sharply at* ABEL *and fixes him with his eyes)*

ABEL   What are you looking at?

BAUER   I'm not looking. I'm wondering.

ABEL   Oh.

BAUER   I'm wondering whether I ought to tell you what I'm wondering about, but I think I'll leave it.

ABEL   Just as you like.

BAUER   So we'll say good-bye for now.

ABEL   Good-bye.

BAUER   The policewoman here will show you where you can collect your belongings. We will keep your brother's dollar bills for the time being. We'll give you a receipt, of course. Good evening, Herr Rosenberg. Good evening, gnädige Frau.

13

The time is five thirty the same afternoon.

The rattling, rusty trolley car is packed with sitting, stand-ing, strap-hanging people on their way home from work. In the wan, flickering light, the swaying bodies with blank, blurred faces look almost like dolls. The air in the overheated car is thick with the smell of wet clothes and dirt.

ABEL and MANUELA are sitting squashed into a corner just behind the front platform. They are tired and silent. ABEL is holding MANUELA's hand. They have just paid their fare—a small yellow stub that is torn off a perforated card.

Suddenly there is a commotion at the far end of the car. A man has climbed onto a seat. He is very fat and red in the face from the exertion. Someone tries to pull him down; others check the attempt.

MAN *(Shouting)*   In this paper you can read what Adolf Hitler has said to his people: "The day has come at last for which our movement was created. The hour for which we have been fighting for years. The moment when the national socialist movement will start its triumphal march for the salvation of Germany. Our movement has been created in order to give the utmost help in the direst need. Now, with this nation watching in dread as the red monster approaches—the stinking Jewish hydra—salvation will come from our movement."

(Someone shouts at the man to shut up. The car brakes suddenly, and the fat man loses his balance and vanishes in the crowd. There is laughter and booing, violent protests, shouts of abuse. Someone screams)

ABEL   What did he say?

MANUELA   He read a speech that someone named Hitler had just made. Hitler said that the hour has struck, that salvation will come to everyone who is afraid, that he will save them, he and his movement.

14

A fire is blazing in the tiled stove and the room is warm. MANUELA *and* ABEL *have even lighted a couple of candles. They have finished eating and drinking and are still sitting at the table. A phonograph with a big horn is playing a well-known tango. Each of them is smoking a small cigar. The coffee is strong and real.*

MANUELA   Do you remember when we got stuck in Damascus, and both Max and I had jaundice?

ABEL   What about it?

MANUELA   We were in a hell of a fix.

ABEL   Yes, I remember.

MANUELA   And what Max did that time?

ABEL   No. Did he do anything special?

MANUELA   I'm going to do what Max did. You draw two columns. At the top of one column you write *Good*, and at the top of the other, *Bad*. Let's start with everything that's bad. Then we'll think of what's good. Get the idea? Don't just sit there sneering. Come on now, Abel. What are the bad things? A whole lot. We're no longer with the circus. Max is dead. Someone has stolen our money. You're miserable, though you don't quite know why. It's November. If we pay the rent, we won't have enough to eat. If we eat properly, we can't pay the rent. What else is bad? People think everything's hopeless. It's catching. People are afraid of being killed, afraid their children will be killed, women are afraid of being raped and tortured. All that's on the bad side. Now for the good side. It's good that you and I can live together and that we've paid the rent in advance for the whole month of November. That's very good. I'll get some more firewood out of that dealer so we won't be cold—that's also good. I've a job—that's the best of the lot. We can make ends meet all November, as the rent's paid. What else is good? *(Pause)* Maybe he's good, that Hitler that everyone's talking about. Though he doesn't like you, of course, because you're a Jew. No, we'll have to cross Hitler off the good side. I can't see why they have to go on at the Jews.

ABEL   I'll tell you why. The Jews are in control of the money. They cheat ordinary people out of their money. All over the world they stick together, amassing all the money that ordinary people have worked to save. Since the Jews get their hands on all the money there is, it's the Jews who are boss. All ordinary people are the Jews' slaves. Ordinary, kind, decent people get tricked by the Jews. At last they go crazy with despair and start hating the Jews. Well, it's only natural, isn't it? The second an ordinary person lays eyes on a Jew, he wants to kill him. It's understandable. Even I can see that, and I'm a Jew myself. The Jews are a poison, something abnormal and diseased, and they should be exterminated. In that column where you've written down all the bad things, you can add that Berlin is filled with Jews—men, women, and children. I'll tell you something else, Manuela, something you won't understand: Frau Holle in there is Jewish. She can tell by looking at me that I'm helpless, out of work, without a chance. She can tell by the look of me, and it frightens me. She also knows—the devil knows how— that I have dollars in my pocket. She diddles me out of some dollars, and I hate her for it and think: "You goddamn hunchbacked Jewish bitch, I could kill you." All the time she talks so sweetly about what a wonderful little person you are and that she feels sorry for you and that you're in danger. Then she threatens me be-

cause she wants to keep you for herself and I've come
between the two of you. So she fleeces me by charging
an exorbitant rent, and I stand there like an idiot.
We're both Jews and we hate each other and exploit
each other, and tomorrow someone might come along
and kill us both and be applauded for doing so. I'll tell
you something else, too: I'm a Jew with a guilty con-
science. Maybe I *am* a parasite, maybe I *am* a goddamn
freak. Maybe it's true, what we're accused of. Deep
down there's a morbid spot sending out signals that I
can't defend myself against. And then I want to go up
to some big, goddamn stupid German policeman and
say: "Please hit me, beat me up, punish me, kill me if
necessary. But punish me so that at last I'm relieved of
the fear that torments me day and night. Hit me hard
so that it hurts. It won't hurt half as much as the evil
I'm forced to live with day in, day out." And when you
hear me talking like this, you know that I'm just as
Jewishly perverted as a Jew should be.

15

*The time is eleven thirty in the evening of Monday, Novem-
ber 5. The garagelike cabaret is full—people are crowded by the
walls and have climbed onto the bar. It is hot, and the air is thick
with tobacco smoke, which cannot overpower the sour smell of
mold and unwashed bodies.*

*All is still. The band produces a wailing pianissimo with
violin and piano. On the platform the main attraction is being
shown—a sex act performed by two thin figures upstage in the
dark, only faintly lighted by the blue and red footlights. One is*

dressed as a man and the other as a woman. Their bodies and movements are shadowy, and now and then they shout obscene words at each other or cry out in feigned lust. Their acting becomes more and more passionate, their panting and the sound of their bodies moving on the soft square bed more and more violent. Then they shout triumphantly, the footlights go out, the curtain is closed with a jerk, the musicians trumpet in relief, and the two artists stand there bowing in the spotlight. They have now changed sex (the girl played the boy and vice versa) and the audience laughs, some applauding and others voicing their disappointment. A tall, thin man in a shabby, purple tuxedo steps forward and begins to sing that life is wonderful, that love is wonderful, but there's no place like home.

Waiters and waitresses, who have been hovering in the background during the previous number, now start weaving between the tables, taking orders. ABEL *pushes his way down toward the stage door. He is sober.*

Then the lights go out. For a few moments the place is in pitch darkness. The manager calls to the audience to keep calm, to stay in their seats. Small flames are already burning here and there. People begin to talk and laugh. The comedian at once takes the stage and, holding a candle, reels off his patter and tells funny stories, each dirtier than the last. His feed, with a candle on his bald head, keeps interrupting him and suggests to the audience that they make use of the dark for their own pleasures. He helpfully promises that the girls at the bar will oblige. Everyone is soon in high spirits.

The passage behind the stage is almost dark. ABEL *makes his way to* MANUELA*'s little dressing room, knocks at the door, and goes in without waiting for an answer. The room is lighted by a single candle.*

MANUELA *is standing by the wall in her song costume. A man gets up from the chair at the dressing table. Although his face is in shadow,* ABEL *recognizes him immediately.*

HANS   I just heard of your brother's death.

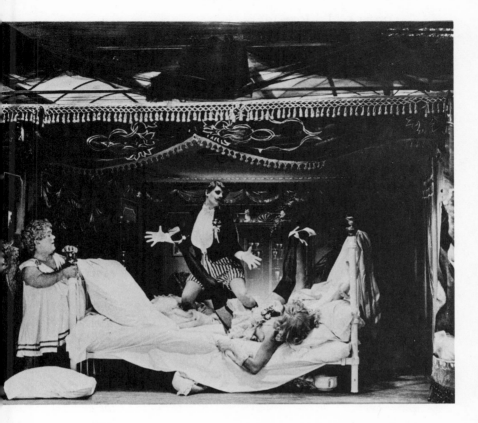

ABEL   What are you doing here?

HANS *(Smiling)*   I dropped in to see Manuela. I hope you
have no objections. I often come here, as a matter of
fact. It sometimes gets a bit lonely for a poor bachelor,
and I live only five minutes from here. I was just
asking Manuela if you and she would like to come back
with me one evening for a glass of wine and a bite of
food.

MANUELA   I'd love to.

ABEL   You can go to hell.

HANS   I won't intrude any longer.

(He says this in an almost meek, apologetic tone. He shakes hands with MANUELA *and bows, then turns to* ABEL *with a smile. When* ABEL *looks away he shrugs regretfully, nods to* MANUELA, *and leaves)*

ABEL   Have you any cigarettes?

MANUELA   On the table.

*(*ABEL *lights a cigarette and sits down on the rickety chair)*

16

They get home about two in the morning and tiptoe through the hall. A light is still burning in FRAU HOLLE*'s room, and they try to avoid attracting her attention.*

FRAU HOLLE   Who is it?

MANUELA   Manuela.

FRAU HOLLE   You have someone with you.

MANUELA   Herr Rosenberg.

FRAU HOLLE   Come in a moment, Manuela.

MANUELA   I'm awfully tired, Frau Holle. Can't we talk tomorrow when I come home to dinner?

FRAU HOLLE   I wish to speak to you now.

(MANUELA *makes a resigned gesture and goes in to* FRAU HOLLE. ABEL *can see her standing at the foot of the bed*)

FRAU HOLLE   I can't sleep for the pain. Besides, I'm worried.

MANUELA   Is it anything to do with me?

FRAU HOLLE   You wouldn't have asked that before, Manuela.

MANUELA   I'm dog-tired, and I think I've caught a cold. I want to go to bed.

FRAU HOLLE   It's about Herr Rosenberg.

MANUELA   Oh?

FRAU HOLLE   I won't have him staying here in my house. He seems unreliable and arrogant. Besides, the authorities don't approve of my letting unmarried couples share a room. I've changed my mind. Herr Rosenberg must move tomorrow.

MANUELA   But he has paid the rent.

FRAU HOLLE   There's the money. I've changed it into marks. It's illegal to have dollars. You ought to know that, Manuela.

MANUELA   If Herr Rosenberg moves, so do I.

FRAU HOLLE   You must do as you like.

MANUELA   We'll move tomorrow.

FRAU HOLLE   There's no hurry as far as you're concerned, Manuela.

MANUELA *(Weeping)*   I think you're horrid. You're nothing but a damned old witch!

(She rushes out of the room, right into ABEL*'s arms. He holds
her tightly while she has a good cry)*

FRAU HOLLE *(Calling)*   Manuela!

MANUELA   Go to hell!

(When they're inside their room, MANUELA *throws her purse
and the large paper bag of money on the table and begins to
pace up and down.* ABEL *sits down on a chair, holding his hat
in both hands.* MANUELA *laughs suddenly, indicating the
table with the dirty dishes still left from dinner)*

MANUELA   I think the column with good things is
shrinking.

*(*ABEL *gets up without answering and begins clearing the
dishes. She goes up to him, stops him, and throws her arms
around him, locking his arms in her embrace)*

MANUELA   We'll manage, you'll see.

*(*ABEL *says nothing)*

MANUELA   As long as we stick together.

ABEL   What was Hans Vergérus doing in your dressing room?

MANUELA *(With a pitiful laugh)*   Not jealous, are you?

ABEL   Have you slept with him?

MANUELA   Yes, I have.

ABEL   Often?

MANUELA *(Upset)*   Don't be silly now, Abel.

ABEL   I want to know.

MANUELA   I think I've slept with him three times. Or maybe it's four. I don't know.

ABEL   Does he pay you?

MANUELA   No. Yes, come to think of it. Once.

ABEL   Why did he pay only once?

MANUELA   I don't know.

ABEL   I want to know.

MANUELA   Maybe I felt sorry for him.

ABEL   Are you in love with him?

MANUELA   I don't know.

ABEL   You don't know?

MANUELA   I feel sorry for him. I'm fond of him. Maybe he needs a little kindness and pampering.

ABEL   Oh! It's like *that*, is it?

MANUELA   Be nice and kind, Abel! Do be nice. It's important that you and I are kind to each other.

(ABEL *makes no answer. They begin to undress, puttering about the room awkwardly and miserably. At last they are lying on the narrow sofa.* MANUELA *turns out the light*)

ABEL   You're all hot. You must have a temperature.

MANUELA   If only I can sleep, it will pass. I'm hardly ever sick.

17

Along the dockside a thin film of ice has formed. It is immediately broken up and swept out on the thick, black water. The heavy, dilapidated buildings crouch in the cold, unheated and full of sleeping, waking, crying, trembling, anxious people. The barracks, the factories, the churches, the railroad stations, the schools, the endless streets, the monuments, and the cemeteries shiver in the bitter wind.

Two policemen, CONSTABLES SCHWARTZ *and* AUERBACH, *are on patrol duty near Brandenburger Tor. They catch sight of a peculiar dark object at the foot of the triumphal arch. They cross the wide, asphalt street and approach the object. They now see that it is a man sitting sprawled against the foundation wall.*

When they come up to him and shine their flashlights on him, they discover that he has no head.

18

On Tuesday, November 6, the newspapers are black with fear, threats, and rumors. The government seems powerless, and a bloody confrontation between the extreme parties appears unavoidable. The same morning there is no longer any milk to be had in Berlin. Many food shops remain closed, as they have nothing to sell. The Reichsmark has practically ceased to exist; the wads of bills are now counted by weight, and no notice is taken of their printed value.

Despite all this, the factory whistles blow, trolley cars and trains rumble through the pouring rain, people go to work, angry office managers tell off unfortunate employees who are late, schoolchildren nod over Xenophon's Anabasis *or grapple with English grammar, housewives scrub their floors and their empty pantries, policemen patrol their beats, businessmen do business, whores ply their trade, actors rehearse, symphony orchestras practice, gravediggers dig, soldiers drill, and doctors diagnose—if they are not operating.*

On this day, several hundred children are born in Berlin, and a somewhat smaller number of people die. The rain never stops, and fear rises like vapor from the asphalt; it can be sensed like a pungent smell. Everyone bears it with him like a nerve poison—a slow-working poison that is felt only as a quicker or slower pulse or a spasm of nausea.

This same morning MANUELA *has overslept. The alarm clock went off, but she fell asleep again. Now she's in a hurry. She drinks a mug of hot coffee standing up, throws on her shabby winter coat, pats* ABEL*'s cheek, and says she'll be home for dinner at two o'clock.*

ABEL *trails her. When he gets down into the street, he sees her running through the rain. She disappears around the corner. He pursues her, and turning into Novemberstrasse, he immediately catches sight of her again. She crosses the street to a small park; in the park is a red brick church surrounded by black, leafless elms.*

ABEL *follows her into the gloom of the church and sees her at once. She has knelt down at the front of the chancel. Morning mass is being held; one or two people are huddled in the pews; and a coughing priest, assisted by a couple of sleepy choirboys, is administering communion. The church is as cold as a burial vault, and the half-burned candles on the altar flicker in the draught.*

When mass is over, the priest hurries into the vestry but leaves the door ajar. The congregation gets up with a scraping of feet and goes out into the rain.

MANUELA *remains kneeling for a few moments. Then she gets up and goes into the vestry, leaving the door open. The two choirboys run noisily down the aisle, their laughter echoing. The priest, in the act of taking off his vestments, comes to the door and shouts to the boys to behave. Then he turns,* MANUELA *says something to him, and the priest answers. He puts on a large black overcoat and his boots.* MANUELA *says something very quietly and he checks himself, then goes farther into the room.*

Under cover of the semi-darkness behind a pillar, ABEL *can see into the vestry: it is a bare room with tall cupboards around the walls and a barred arched window. In the middle of the floor is a battered table. The priest has just sat down with his back to the door.* MANUELA *is standing on the other side of the table.* ABEL *can clearly see her face illuminated by the four naked bulbs of the ceiling light. She is standing bent forward with her eyes lowered. Her face is ashen gray, her eyelids are red and swollen, and she shakes her head. The priest coughs and blows his nose.*

MANUELA   I don't know why I come here bothering you. I've never taken much notice of God, and I don't think God has taken much notice of me either. I've never gone to church. I don't think I was even christened— my father was a confirmed atheist and I believed as he did. No.

(She thinks back, puts her hands together, raises her eyes, and looks at the priest, then shakes her head once more)

MANUELA   My name's MANUELA. My father's some kind of magician; I haven't seen him for many years. My mother was a circus rider. I've lived all my life with various circuses. My husband, who's dead, was also a circus artist. *(Weeps)* I'm sorry to cry, but I seem to have the flu—I feel so dizzy and peculiar and cry for

no reason. *(Pause)* No, I'm not a timid person. I've always thought I had a good life. Come to think of it, I've never even considered whether life was good or bad.

(The priest says nothing. He sits hunched in his big winter overcoat, coughing now and then. MANUELA *looks around her anxiously, as if her courage has suddenly failed her)*

MANUELA   Maybe it was all wrong of me to trouble you. But I must talk to someone who understands. This last week I've come here to morning mass because I've been so bewildered. Then I heard someone say that you were American, despite your German name. It felt comforting, as my German isn't very good.

PRIEST   My dear young lady, please come to the point. I have a service shortly.

MANUELA   Yes. No. I see.

PRIEST   Maybe you'll come back?

(He gets up quickly and tucks in his scarf. MANUELA *remains standing at the end of the table. Her face expresses despair and bewilderment)*

MANUELA   I'm sorry to have detained you.

PRIEST   Don't mention it.

*(*MANUELA *goes slowly toward the door, dragging her feet. She is fighting down her tears)*

MANUELA   All I want to do is cry.

PRIEST   Let's be brave now.

MANUELA *(Faintly)*   All the guilt is too much for me.

(MANUELA *sits down on a chair by the wall. The priest stands in front of her. He glances at the wall clock and shows his impatience)*

MANUELA   I feel it's my fault that Max committed suicide. I knew all along that something would happen to him. When his brother came and told me that Max had shot himself, I felt nothing. Relief, if anything. Then came that funny feeling. I don't understand it; I've never felt it before. You're responsible for someone and you fail in your duty, and there you stand, empty-handed and ashamed, going over and over in your mind what you should have done.

(*The priest has sat down on a stool opposite* MANUELA. *He has taken off his glasses and is wiping them carefully with a spotless handkerchief)*

MANUELA   And now I feel I have to take care of his brother, and that's the worst of it.

PRIEST   The worst of it?

MANUELA   He's just like Max. He doesn't say what he thinks. He just charges ahead with all his feelings. He looks so frightened all the time. I try to tell him that we'll help each other, but it's just words to him. He seems to think that everything I say is useless and that fear is the only real thing. And I'm sick, what's more. I don't know what's wrong with me. Is there no forgiveness?

PRIEST   For the believer there is forgiveness.

MANUELA   But what is there for those who don't believe?

PRIEST   Would you like me to pray for you?

(The tired, overworked man has stopped for a moment. He puts out his hand and touches her shoulder in a clumsy, consoling gesture. She looks at him in surprise. He turns his eyes away immediately)

MANUELA   Do you think it would help?

PRIEST   I don't know.

MANUELA   Now?

PRIEST   Yes. Now.

(He kneels down on the stone floor. MANUELA *hesitates, then follows his example. The priest clasps his hands)*

MANUELA   Is it any special prayer?

PRIEST   Quiet. I must think. *(Pause)* We live far away from God, so far away that no doubt He doesn't hear us when we pray to Him for help. So we must help each other. We must give each other the forgiveness that a remote God denies us. I say to you that you are forgiven for your husband's death. You are no longer to blame. I beg your forgiveness for my apathy and indifference. Do you forgive me?

MANUELA *(Softly)*   Yes.

PRIEST   This is all we can do.

(He stands up and brushes the dust off his pants and coat. MANUELA *also gets up)*

PRIEST Now I must hurry. The parish priest is always punctual, and he gets annoyed if one is late.

(They hurry through the church, the priest already ahead. ABEL *moves farther into the darkness behind the pillar. When* MANUELA *has disappeared, he continues to follow her)*

19

ABEL *follows* MANUELA *at a distance. They come out onto a street lined by six-story apartment houses. Just beyond the gray buildings is a glimpse of St. Anna's Clinic, enclosed by high iron railings.* MANUELA *opens the street door of Number 28. She enters a dark vestibule with gleaming handrails and marble stairs, turns to the left, opens another door, and comes out into the yard, which is like a well and separated from other yards by a high wall.* ABEL *follows her into the dingy entrance of the back building. She stops in front of a door with no name on it and fumbles in her purse. She finds a key and unlocks the door, leaving it open behind her.*

ABEL *enters and stands in a long passage that ends in a big kitchen. Leading off the kitchen is another room.* MANUELA *stands in the inner room. The rain is pattering against the grimy windows. She holds her head forward like a frightened animal. Taking off her coat slowly, she turns and catches sight of* ABEL.

ABEL   What the hell's the meaning of this?

MANUELA   We're going to live here, you and I. Isn't it nice?

(Her tone is sad and appealing. He takes a few steps into the kitchen, then walks into the inner room. She touches his hand and looks at him as if trying to allay his suspicions.

The room is cramped and square, with big patches of mold on the ceiling. A cumbersome, shiny black wardrobe takes up one wall, and by the other is a sofa, which can be made into a double bed. By the window is a brown table, with four high-backed chairs. The wallpaper is elaborately patterned, and the walls are adorned with a few mournfully romantic pictures. To the left of the huge wardrobe hangs a mirror with a beveled edge in a darkened-gold frame, and above the sofa ticks an ornate wall clock. By the right wall stand a couple of shabby leather armchairs and a low, round table with a copper top. On the dirty floorboards is an Oriental rug with part of the pattern worn away. Unlike the cluttered living room, the kitchen is fairly spacious and equipped with gas cooker, sink and cold-water faucet high up on the wall, a large pantry, an icebox, a long shelf with various pots and pans, a round, wooden table by the window with three chairs, an electric lamp with long fringes hanging from the ceiling, and fairly unworn linoleum on the floor. In the dark hall is a high coal stove, with a full coal box beside it. The apartment seems to have been occupied by someone forced to move from a solid middle-class home to this cramped environment, which looks out onto a dirty, yellow wall)

MANUELA   When you came to the cabaret yesterday, I had just been telling Hans Vergérus of our difficulties. He immediately suggested that we move into this apartment which he, or rather St. Anna's Clinic, has the use of and which had just become vacant. Do say it's nice! We needn't pay any rent for the time being. He also said that you could work in the clinic's archives. Wouldn't that be nice, Abel? We could live here until we've decided about the future. Please say it would be nice!

ABEL   I'm damned if I'm going to live here or accept any favors from that blasted Vergérus!

(MANUELA *doesn't answer. She sits down at the big table on one of the high-backed chairs and props her head in her hands. She is very tired*)

ABEL   It's much better if we each go our own way.

(MANUELA *doesn't answer now either. She sits gazing at the wall outside the window and at the streaks made by the rain on the dirty windows*)

ABEL   You have no obligations as far as I'm concerned.

(MANUELA *still says nothing. She covers her face with her hands and lets her head drop, but she is not crying. She doesn't utter a sound.* ABEL *goes into the kitchen and stands there, hesitating*)

ABEL   I probably won't be seeing you for a while. It's much better not to muddle everything up.

MANUELA   I see.

(ABEL *leaves the door open, goes down the stairs, and comes out into the well-like yard. The rain has filled the drains, which are overflowing with putrid waste water. He stops, looks up at the window, and glimpses* MANUELA*'s ashen-gray face behind the pane as she stands looking down at him.*

Suddenly he gives in, turns back, runs up the stairs, meets her in the hall, and throws his arms around her. She takes his head between her hands and kisses him on the lips)

20

That same evening the cabaret Zum Blauen Esel is raided by the police. The time is around eleven, and MANUELA, *looking wretched, is singing in a faint voice that she has some candy. Because of the pouring rain, the place is half empty. The smell of mold is stronger than ever, and the same dank chill is everywhere. The scantily clad girls at the bar have put on woollies and shawls; and one of them, as she serves the drinks, is wrapped in*

a threadbare man's overcoat. ABEL *is greeted by the whores
sitting at the entrance waiting for customers. He is soaking wet
and takes off his overcoat; the old man in the cloakroom says he
will hang it up to dry.* ABEL *thanks him and makes his way
through the room. He sits at a table and lights the stub of a
cigarette. The manager comes up to him with a glass of beer and
sits down beside him. He is a small man with dyed hair, anxious
darting eyes, and a dark, madeup face with thick glasses. On his
left forefinger he wears an obviously costly ring.*

SOLOMON How do you like my English accent? I lived
for some years with a woman fakir from New Jersey.
She taught me all the English I know. There's no point
in continuing here in Berlin. Look around you, Herr
Rosenberg! Thirty-six people! And what a program!
Manuela is not good. I don't know what's the matter
with her this evening; she seems worse than usual.

ABEL She has the flu.

SOLOMON What do you think, Herr Rosenberg? A cabaret with a brothel in Beirut, for example? A totally
different climate, a totally different appreciation.
We'll close earlier tonight and shorten the program.
It's useless staying open. I've never seen anything like
this rain. Maybe it's the Flood. Cheers, Herr Rosenberg.

*(He is about to get up when the entrance doors crash open. A
girl screams in anger and pain; someone shouts an order. The
front part of the room is suddenly filled with men in shiny
raincoats, jackboots, and military caps. They are armed with
truncheons.*
  SOLOMON*'s dark face first flushes and then withers up. He
stands up with a cigarette in his right hand and the glass in*

his left. He gives ABEL *a peculiar smile and shrinks inside his
immaculate tuxedo)*

SOLOMON   I've been expecting this.

*(Four of the men have forced their way up onto the stage. One
of them has grabbed* MANUELA *by the wrist and is holding her
in a tight grip. The audience has stood up; some of them are
arguing angrily by the door. The musicians are crowded in
a corner of the orchestra pit.*

    *Suddenly the lights go up. A boy reads out a resolution in
which several times he utters the words "in the name of the
German people." When he has finished reading, a fat man,
who seems to be the leader of the group, asks where the manager is.* SOLOMON *sits down and says nothing. One of the girls
at the bar points to him and says, "There he is, the Jewish
swine." The leader goes up to the table)*

LEADER   I don't like your nose. Take off your glasses, if
you don't want them broken.

*(*SOLOMON *obeys immediately. The leader seizes him by his
thin, dyed hair and bangs his face against the tabletop. After
a minute or so of this treatment,* SOLOMON*'s features are a
gory pulp. All this happens without anyone moving.* ABEL
*remains seated where he is. Blood spatters on his jacket and
pants, but he cannot move. Unable even to turn his head
away, he watches* SOLOMON*'s face being transformed.*

    *When the leader considers that the manager has had enough
punishment, he blows a whistle. It's the signal for violent
activity. The uniformed men set about ravaging the cabaret
and assaulting the guests, the musicians, and the artists. For
a while there is tumult. Then two short signals are heard from
the whistle. The wrecking stops and the men head toward the
exit. In no time they have all vanished. Some cars are started
up and driven off down the empty, rain-flooded street. Inside*

*the cabaret, the furniture and décor are smashed and people
are injured.* ABEL, *who has been lying under a table, has been
hit over the ear with a truncheon. He is bleeding heavily, but
it is only a surface wound. He begins to hunt for* MANUELA
*among the injured, sobbing, and terrified people. He finds her
almost at once. She is unhurt and helps* SOLOMON *bind nap-
kins around his battered face.*

*A rough fight is going on in a corner between the girl who
pointed out the manager and two girls who stood up for him)*

MANUELA   That boy who grabbed me on the stage was
kind. He whispered that he'd only pretend to lay into
me and that I was to scream bloody murder. I did, too.

21

*They spend the first night in their new refuge among suitcases
still unpacked and undefined objects from* MANUELA*'s former
life.* ABEL *can't sleep. He is half sitting up in the pulled-out sofa
bed, smoking.* MANUELA *sleeps heavily but restlessly. She has a
temperature.*

*Beside the bed is a standard lamp with a wobbly base and a
brown cloth shade. It is covered with a shawl and sheds a soft,
shadowless light over the room.*

It is still raining.

*Now and then through the stillness a heavy engine can be
heard. It makes the building vibrate. The dull throb ends as
abruptly as it begins.* ABEL *listens involuntarily to the unsteady
rhythm.*

MANUELA *wakes up and looks around her.*

MANUELA   Can't you sleep?

ABEL   I have to be drunk before I can sleep.

MANUELA   There's half a bottle of gin over there in the small suitcase. As I don't like gin, it hasn't been opened.

(ABEL *immediately hunts about until he finds the bottle and gets a glass from the kitchen. He pours out a stiff dram and swallows it in one gulp, standing in the middle of the room in a tattered, old terry cloth bathrobe. He pours out more gin, almost a full glass, and drinks it. It calms him down somewhat. He sits on the edge of the sofa bed*)

ABEL   You don't look too good.

MANUELA   It's nice having a temperature, actually. You daydream, fall asleep, wake up, mix everything up. Suddenly I'm six years old, then I'm fifteen. It's all so clear.

ABEL   Can you hear that engine? It's starting up again.

MANUELA   What engine?

ABEL   Can't you hear it?

MANUELA   There's something rumbling.

ABEL   Yes. An engine.

MANUELA   I remember sitting in the sun watching poor Papa practicing a new number. It wouldn't go right. Mama came out of the wagon and said, "It's better if you do it this way." And she showed him what to do. He stood there looking embarrassed, with a stoop and a sheepish smile, dressed in a green-and-white striped jacket. *(Pause)* It's like being on an island.

ABEL *(Drinking)*   Oh.

MANUELA   I don't know. It's hard to describe. Our boat sank and we very nearly drowned. The people around us disappeared. And then look what happened at the cabaret tonight.

ABEL   It's damned awful with that engine. Don't you think so, too?

MANUELA   No.

ABEL   Tomorrow I'll find out what it is.

MANUELA   Do you know what's hardest of all?

ABEL *(Drinking)*   No.

MANUELA   The fact that people have no future. It's not just you and I who haven't much to look forward to. Everyone has lost his future.

ABEL   I don't give a damn about the past, and I don't give a damn about the future either. I'm satisfied—I'm getting drunk at last.

MANUELA   We haven't any words either. As long as you can hope and look forward, you don't need words. But as it is now, it's terrible that people haven't any language. All they have is a scream or a fit of rage or weeping. *(Pause)* Those who can say the words and put a name to their feelings have all the power.

ABEL   Have you made all that up yourself?

MANUELA   No.

ABEL   Was it Hans Vergérus?

MANUELA   I think so. He also said, "If those who give words to people's feelings like people, it's all right. If they hate people . . ."

(She breaks off and lays the back of her hand on her brow and moistens her lips)

ABEL   It's better not to know.

MANUELA   That old bathrobe you're using as pajamas. It was Papa's. Goddamn touching, isn't it?

(ABEL *doesn't hear. He has fallen asleep at last, propped against the back of the sofa bed with the empty bottle in his hand. He has dropped the glass. His mouth is half open, his face sallow, slack, and childlike.* MANUELA *looks at him for a while. Then she carefully takes the bottle from him, puts it on the floor, gets out of bed, and puts out the lamp. The room is in almost total darkness. Gradually the rectangle of the window appears, streaked with rain. She can also make out the wall dividing the yard.*

The engine is quiet at last.

Then a scream is heard, faint and far away. Then another. It is a man screaming in mortal dread. ABEL *at once opens his eyes and listens. But now all is silent. Only the rain can be heard)*

22

An old man with a courtly manner, well-groomed white hair, and childlike blue eyes behind gold-rimmed glasses bids ABEL *welcome to the archives, a large basement room beneath the clinic's sprawling building.*

SOLTERMANN How do you do, Herr Rosenberg? I'm pleased to meet you. May I introduce myself: Dr. Soltermann. This is my colleague, Dr. Fuchs. We are in charge of the archives of St. Anna's Clinic—the largest hospital archives in Europe and one of the largest in the world. We have a floor space of several thousand square meters, Herr Rosenberg! And our card index comprises over a hundred thousand entries. But then

St. Anna's Clinic has been in existence for three hundred and fifty-seven years. In various guises, of course. Dr. Fuchs and I are very grateful to have an assistant at last. We have been complaining to our head, Professor Vergérus, for years, all to no avail. Please feel that you are very welcome, Herr Rosenberg.

FUCHS *(With a thick accent)* Don't you think that Dr. Soltermann speaks very good English?

ABEL Very good!

SOLTERMANN Dr. Fuchs is far too kind. I spent seven years in England before the war. My doctor's thesis dealt with the erotic perversions in the writings of Ben Jonson. An interesting but limited subject.

(DR. SOLTERMANN boasts modestly, at the same time finding it hard to curb his delight. DR. FUCHS, who accompanies them down the long passage between endless shelves to the ceiling, makes encouraging little exclamations and comments)

SOLTERMANN May I ask, Herr Rosenberg, if you have any previous experience in archive work?

ABEL No, unfortunately I've never—

SOLTERMANN I was afraid so. But never mind. This very day I can give you a responsible task that calls for very little archive routine.

ABEL *(Smiling)* I am very grateful.

SOLTERMANN Dr. Fuchs and I have discussed the matter and are agreed.

FUCHS   Yes.

(During this conversation they have penetrated a labyrinth of passages and shelves, opening and closing doors. They now stop in a rectangular room with small windows just below the ceiling. A desk is poked into one corner and a hanging carbon-filament lamp sheds a feeble light)

SOLTERMANN   This will be your place, Herr Rosenberg. We begin work each morning at eight o'clock and finish at six. We have dinner at one thirty. We take it in turns, fetching it from the kitchen of the clinic. The dinner break is half an hour. We are also entitled to take home our supper in a special container—these days that is a priceless emolument. You will find other rules on the bulletin board above your desk. You will be paid your weekly salary each Friday at the cashier's office of the clinic. When the time comes, I will go with you and show you the ropes. Good morning, Herr Rosenberg.

ABEL   *(Dismayed)*   Forgive my asking, but what am I to do?

(DR. SOLTERMANN laughs loudly and DR. FUCHS smiles. They turn back, instructing and demonstrating)

SOLTERMANN   You see those rows of brown files on the right-hand shelf? They are very valuable, and we take very great care of them. Over there to the left you will see yellow files of a cheaper kind. Your first task will be to remove the contents of the brown files and trans-fer them to the yellow files, after which you will num-ber and letter them in the same way as the brown ones.

ABEL   And what am I to do with the brown files?

SOLTERMANN   You will place them where the yellow files were before. Good luck, Herr Rosenberg.

(DR. SOLTERMANN *puts out a dry and very cold hand.* DR. FUCHS *also takes leave in the same ceremonious manner*)

ABEL   How shall I find my way out?

SOLTERMANN   At dinner time either Dr. Fuchs or I will come for you. You can rely on us. We won't forget you. *(He laughs, then grows solemn)* By the way, one thing I nearly forgot. It won't do any harm for me to point out that all the material in this room is strictly confidential. It must not be taken out of here, and you must not read or try to decipher the documents that pass through your hands. Our clinic has a great humanistic tradition, Herr Rosenberg, and reverence for humanity has always been our law. All the brown files are full of reports of inconceivable human suffering, of the battles of science, its victories and defeats. Here are unheard-of disclosures of human nature's most inaccessible secrets.

ABEL   Have you read those files yourself?

SOLTERMANN   Naturally. I have read everything in our archives. Have I not, Dr. Fuchs?

(DR. FUCHS *nods in agreement.*
    The two men withdraw, closing the big iron door behind them. ABEL *hears their footsteps die away in the passage. He is left alone in this room, which seems to him hermetic. He fights off the unpleasant feeling of being shut in, puts on the gray working coat that hangs by the bulletin board, and begins his work.*
    He discovers at once that each file contains thinner files. On

each of these is a combined figure and letter code. He opens one of the thin files cautiously. It contains a bundle of closely typed pages fastened together. On each front page is a name and some data, as well as three photographs, two in profile and one full face. For the rest, the pages contain long accounts in German and Latin, interspersed with dates)

23

During the dinner break, ABEL *finds his way outside to the hospital laundry, which is housed in a square brick building near the boiler room with its tall chimney. Steam is forced out through ventilators in the high, misty windows and dispersed in the cold wind. Behind the panes, white-clad women can be glimpsed in constant movement. Mounds of dirty linen are piled on long trolleys. A large spin-drier emits a deafening noise. The floor is covered with wet duckboards.*

MANUELA *catches sight of* ABEL *and signals him to go to the back door. She is waiting for him, not daring to ask him into the cramped, green-painted anteroom. She stands in the high, narrow doorway with a cigarette in her hand. She is wearing white overalls and a large, protective apron of sacking. On her head she has a white cloth and on her feet, clogs. Her face is flushed and her eyes are dull with temperature.*

ABEL   How's it going?

MANUELA   It's terribly heavy work.

ABEL   You're not well.

MANUELA   No.

ABEL   Have you had anything to eat?

MANUELA   We have dinner in the hospital staff dining room.

ABEL   When do you knock off?

MANUELA   I think I can go at seven.

ABEL   I'm allowed to take supper from the kitchen. It's part of the salary.

MANUELA How are you getting on in the archives?

ABEL Fine.

MANUELA I don't think I dare stand here any longer. Everything's awfully strict.

ABEL Manuela!

MANUELA Yes?

ABEL You look so thin and ill. *(Helpless in his sudden tenderness)* I wish I could—

MANUELA I'm all right, Abel. It might be worse. I must hurry now. We must get out your winter coat. You'll freeze to death if you go around all winter in that.

ABEL Can't you say you're sick?

MANUELA I don't dare.

(She looks around and gives a timid smile. A fat woman with a puffy face comes up behind her. MANUELA *takes her hand from the door and turns into the room. The woman pours out a stream of words, her face dark with anger. She grabs* MANUELA *by the arm and pushes her into a corner.*

ABEL returns at a run to the archives. He turns a corner, crouching in the cutting wind. A cloud of dust whips his face. Someone takes him gently by the arm and he looks up. It is HANS VERGÉRUS *in a fur-trimmed winter coat and a fur hat. A car drives past)*

HANS You were nearly run over.

ABEL   Thanks.

HANS   How do you like it here with us?

ABEL   I've only just started.

HANS   And Manuela?

ABEL   You can ask her yourself.

HANS   Let's meet one evening all three. Eh?

   (ABEL *says nothing;* HANS *says nothing*)

ABEL   Excuse me, I'm in rather a hurry.

HANS   Why, of course. I'll be seeing you.

   (ABEL *hurries on, fighting down a violent dread*)

24

DR. FUCHS *shows him the way through the labyrinth of the archives.*

FUCHS   Dr. Soltermann went home after dinner. He is in poor health. I am usually alone here nowadays.

   (*Suddenly he stops and turns his worried little face to* ABEL, *who is also forced to stop.* DR. FUCHS's *eyes are large and bright, a trifle colorless; the thin, gray hair lies in curls around the high dome of the head; the nose is long and narrow; the mouth is pursed with anxiety)*

FUCHS Now that Dr. Soltermann is gone, I can say it. *(Whispering)* Something horrible is going on here.

ABEL Where?

FUCHS Here. At the clinic.

ABEL At the clinic?

(DR. FUCHS nods and looks about him as though someone might be eavesdropping behind a shelf. Taking ABEL by the hand, he leads him through a side passage into a small room, unlocking the narrow green-painted door with a key from his large bunch. He switches on an unshaded bulb and goes up to a shelf. After searching for a moment, he takes down a gray file full of documents tied with string. He spreads them out on the table and looks expectantly at ABEL)

FUCHS Do you know what these are, Herr Rosenberg?

ABEL I don't understand German.

FUCHS They are reports, detailed reports. Marked secret.

ABEL Well?

FUCHS Reports concerning certain experiments undertaken at the clinic under the supervision of Professor Vergérus.

ABEL I don't understand.

FUCHS   Can you guess what kind of experiments, Herr Rosenberg?

ABEL   No, not possibly.

FUCHS   Very strange experiments . . .

ABEL   Oh?

FUCHS   Experiments with human beings, Herr Rosenberg.

25

When ABEL *comes out from the archives after the day's work it is dark, but bright lamps light up the various yards of the hospital and the main entrance.* DR. FUCHS *turns up the collar of his overcoat and raises his hat. His glasses shine and the thin, curly hair blows in the wind. He says a polite "auf Wiedersehen" and hurries off toward the trolley-car stop. Dark, crouching shadows hover around the main entrance.* ABEL *lights his next to last cigarette and begins looking for the hospital kitchen, which is a long building standing by itself in one of the inner courtyards. He finds a line of about a hundred people shuffling in toward a long counter. They are all carrying food containers. When they reach the counter, they show their passes and are checked off on a list. It is all done quickly, and after a short wait* ABEL *is facing the woman behind the counter. He shows his pass, which is checked on the list. The woman hands his pass back, shaking her head and explaining in German that he must go to another counter farther away. By degrees he understands what*

*she means. A man behind him in the line congratulates him in
English with hardly any accent, saying that the food at the other
counter is better.* ABEL *smiles politely and goes to the other
counter, which is connected to the hospital staff dining room. At
this time of day, it is almost empty; one or two nurses are sitting
at a table, talking quietly.* ABEL *shows his pass again. The
woman studies it carefully, then nods encouragingly and hurries
over to a large warming cupboard. She opens the door and lifts
out a double container, which she puts on the counter. Then she
notes on her list that it has been picked up, explaining in German
to* ABEL *that he is to come to her counter every day. She points
to his name on the lid of the container, and he says that he
understands.*

26

MANUELA *and* ABEL *eat in silence—a soup made of potatoes and cabbage, with a few lumps of overboiled meat at the bottom. With it they chew black bread and lard.*

ABEL   That engine is driving me mad.

MANUELA   I didn't notice it.

ABEL   Surely you can hear it!

MANUELA   Yes, now that you mention it.

ABEL   It's so damned hot in here. Can't we open a window?

MANUELA   I think you can open the window on the right in the kitchen.

(ABEL *gets up roughly from the table and goes into the kitchen. He flings open the only window that isn't sealed up. He lights his last cigarette and stands at the window staring out at the yellow wall of the yard.* MANUELA *remains sitting at the table. She has finished eating)*

ABEL   I have a blasted headache.

MANUELA   I think I've a powder somewhere.

ABEL   It's like a trap.

MANUELA   What is?

ABEL *(Shouting)*   Don't be an idiot! Can't you feel that we're shut in? My heart feels as if it will jump out of my body, the way it's pounding.

MANUELA   Don't get hysterical, Abel.

(He swings round to answer her but checks himself. She is looking at him in such distress that he forgets the violent words)

MANUELA   If we panic, we're done for.

ABEL   Yes.

MANUELA   We must get back to the circus somehow. We must find someone to take Max's place or else think up a new number that we can do, just the two of us. It shouldn't be impossible. I've been turning it over in my mind. You stand here, and I here, and we meet over a trapeze. We could work without a safety net— it has many advantages. I can speak to Hollinger if you wish. He likes me. We'll do it just for our keep while we practice the number. I'm sure we can get our old wagon back, and we can lend a hand in the stables.

(ABEL doesn't answer. He has started to pace up and down between the kitchen and the living room, out into the hall and back again. MANUELA shuts her eyes and presses her lips together)

ABEL My head's aching.

MANUELA So you said just now.

ABEL Are you sure the gas isn't leaking?

MANUELA No, it's not leaking.

ABEL How can you be so sure?

MANUELA Because I tried it.

ABEL So you did think it was leaking?

MANUELA Yes, because I have a headache, too. You're going on like a lunatic. You can leave if you don't want to stay.

ABEL So you're turning me out.

MANUELA I simply mean that you can go where you like. You've no obligations toward me and I've no obligations toward you. I've done what I could to keep us going; now I can't go on. *(Shouts)* Do you hear? I can't go on. I don't give a damn about your fear. I don't give a damn about you.

ABEL So you want me to go?

MANUELA No.

ABEL Poor Manuela.

MANUELA Are you being nice now? Or sarcastic?

(She gets up from the table and holds out her skinny arms. He takes a step toward her, draws her to him, and they stand for a long time in an embrace. Suddenly they begin to kiss each other and fall onto the bed)

ABEL I can't.

MANUELA We'll just lie with our arms around each other.

ABEL No, I can't.

MANUELA Just lie still. It's lovely.

(They hold each other tightly. She stretches out her arm and pulls out the plug of the bedside lamp. The light from the kitchen makes a rectangle on the opposite wall. They can see each other's faces faintly in the semi-darkness)

ABEL No, I can't lie like this.

MANUELA *(Pleading)* Just for a little while.

(She holds on to him. Slowly the tension in his body eases, he closes his eyes, and his head rests heavily on her shoulder. Then the dull, distant sound of the engine is heard.

ABEL wrenches himself free of MANUELA's embrace and sits up. He puts his hands to his face, takes them away immediately, shakes his head, and gets up. He goes into the hall and puts on his coat, comes back, stands irresolutely in the doorway. He can see MANUELA sitting on the bed with her head bent down. He wants to say something to her but can't find the words. MANUELA, too, is mute.

He leaves the house at a run)

27

By the night of Wednesday, November 7, the government has mobilized some emergency troops for the defense of Berlin. The wild and totally uncontrollable rumors and counter-rumors have culminated in a storm, followed by a brooding, expectant silence. The city's administrative centers and the main streets are patrolled by soldiers; otherwise, there are no outward signs. Still more food stores and warehouses have closed down for lack of goods. For two days no work has been done at the wharves because of a strike. During certain hours of the day, the electricity is cut off. Deliveries of coal to gasworks and households have practically ceased. In this creeping paralysis, night life burns like a hectic fever, an isolated world of heat deep inside a dying organism.

28

ABEL has made his way to a bar near the Kurfürstendamm. It is packed with people who have just streamed out of theaters and movie houses. He shows his remaining dollar at the counter and is immediately given a glass of brandy, then a second and a third. In the middle of the floor is a tiny circular space where people, all pressed together, are trying to dance. Four black men are playing jazz; a harsh light falls over their sweaty, slack faces. ABEL *pays with his dollar and has a thick wad of bills thrust into his hand.*

He wanders aimlessly through the back streets parallel to the Kurfürstendamm. It is darker here, with hardly any traffic. Trucks with soldiers rumble past; a girl tugs at his sleeve and offers her services in a shrill and pleading voice. He shakes her off and goes on, half running.

He turns a corner and stops in confusion. His heart is pounding; he has a splitting headache and feels drunk and wretched. The street has been partly taken up. On the other side is an insignificant little shop that sells needlework, sewing cottons, and knitting wools. On the window, in neat white letters, is A. ROSENBERG—NEEDLEWORK. ABEL *crosses the street, avoiding a*

*heap of paving stones, and stares at the faintly lighted window
with its display of colorful tablecloths, cushions, embroidery,
and skeins of wool. He reads the text over and over:* A. ROSEN-
BERG—NEEDLEWORK. *A door opens inside the darkness of the
shop, and a tall elderly man is outlined against the bright
rectangle. Then a woman appears, thin, rather bent, with thick,
dark hair in a knob on top of her head. The man has two account
books under his arm, and the woman is carrying a basket. They
are talking, but* ABEL *cannot hear what they say.*

On a sudden impulse ABEL *picks up a paving stone and hurls
it at the window, which shatters with a loud crash. The woman
gives a short scream and points to* ABEL. *The man throws the
books on the counter and rushes to the door. He fumbles at it and
gets it open.* ABEL *stands quite still, awaiting the man's fury
with rising excitement. Without a word the man throws himself
at* ABEL, *shakes him, then lets him go to give him a chance to
defend himself. But* ABEL *doesn't move. Time and again he is
struck in the face; the woman tears his hair and scratches his
neck. The man punches him in the chest, and he loses his balance,
falling against the heap of paving stones. Then he sees that a
crowd has gathered to witness the spectacle. The man drags* ABEL
*to his feet, swings him around, and presses him against the wall.
He has lost his glasses, and the light from the window falls across
his face.* ABEL *can feel his breath, which smells strongly of
Turkish tobacco. The big, gray eyes are staring and full of tears;
the wide mouth trembles, uttering inaudible words. The woman
behind him appeals to the bystanders to call the police.* ABEL *feels
a burning pain as the man keeps hitting his face. Suddenly* ABEL
*raises his arms and grips the man's wrists, holding him in a vise.
His expression changes from fury to fear as* ABEL *slowly forces
him to his knees. Then he lets him go and walks away. The
woman pursues him, shouting abuse and clinging to him. He is
forced to stop and turn toward her. The thick, dark hair has
come loose and falls over her shoulders; the thin, angry face is
close to his and she spits at him. He puts one arm around her
waist and presses her against him, gripping the thick hair with*

his other hand. Then he bends forward and kisses the thin, angry mouth. He holds her lips pressed against his in a long kiss, then he frees himself and pushes her away. She screams with rage and falls to the sidewalk. ABEL *takes to his heels, turns into another street, and stops. He has to support himself against the wall of a house. Time and again he is shaken by inner convulsions.*

29

A girl stops and looks at him attentively. He tells her to go away. She says she speaks English. He says he's not interested. She replies that he looks sick. He tells her to go to hell. She laughs and says they are there already. ABEL *raises his head and looks at her. She is short and has a round, rather flabby face with heavily madeup dark-blue eyes. She is wearing a half-length leather jacket with a belt and a fur collar. A vivid-green cloche hat is pulled down over the dyed, shingled hair. She takes him by the arm and leads him across the street into a side alley, through an archway, and into a dimly lighted yard stinking of urine. She unlocks a red-painted door with broken panes and leads him up a steep wooden staircase, where a few weak light bulbs shine down on peeling doors and broken handrails. On the fourth floor she stops and unlocks a door, pushing him ahead of her through a curtain. They are standing in a narrow passage. On one side is a table covered with a stained oilcloth, on which are a spirit stove and a few empty cans and saucepans. Coats are hanging on the other side. A narrow, half-open door leads to an adjoining room, from which gramophonic music and a dim pink light are issuing. The girl knocks at the door and, without waiting for an answer, takes* ABEL*'s hand and draws him inside.*

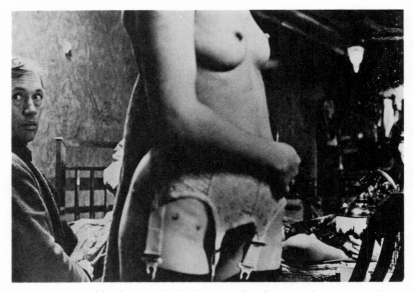

A young black man is sitting on the floor, naked except for an orange-colored jacket. A lanky girl with large breasts and slender hips is sprawling on the unmade bed. She has wrapped an Oriental shawl around her. Her face has an unhealthy pallor and she laughs raucously. The black man starts pouring out a stream of words.

MONROE   She says I can't fuck. She can't talk—she has fangs in her cunt. Mikaela, tell her she doesn't know what she's talking about. Please tell that lousy woman on the bed that you and I have screwed at least fifteen times.

MIKAELA   My name's Mikaela.

STELLA *(Shrieking with laughter)*   That black cocksucker's crazy! If you have a customer, Monroe and I can go into my room, though it's much warmer here. Do you like incense? It's real Indonesian, guaranteed erotic.

MIKAELA *(To Abel)* Take your coat off.

ABEL No thanks.

(He sits down in a low, sagging armchair near the door)

MONROE *(Shrilly)* Stella's a goddamn cruel person. Everyone says so. No one's as spiteful as you are. I was told that only yesterday. You're plain crazy.

STELLA Mikaela, you know me and you know Monroe. You know quite well he can only fuck faggots, and if you say he's only *half* screwed you, then you're lying.

MIKAELA Is there any left?

STELLA There's some in the drawer. I saved it for you.

MIKAELA *(Good-naturedly)* Nice of you, seeing it was mine.

MONROE Do you remember that time you'd been to the hospital because they thought you had syphilis? Who was kind and lay in your bed every night to comfort you and risked catching it?

STELLA *(Shouting)* But I didn't have syphilis, damn you!

MONROE You thought you had. You looked lousy. You *are* lousy. Everyone says you're the worst tart on the whole of Steinstrasse.

(The Gramophone has stopped playing and is rasping in its empty groove. MONROE winds it up and turns the record over. MIKAELA has taken a small glass bottle out of the drawer of the bedside table. It contains a thin layer of white powder. She

carefully pours a few grains onto her forefinger, puts it to her nose, and inhales)

MIKAELA   Like some? It's nice.

(ABEL *shakes his head)*
    (MIKAELA *gets undressed, flinging her clothes down any-where. She steps over* MONROE, *who kisses her on the bottom, opens a cupboard, gets out a pea-green kimono, and looks at herself in the mirror, studying the white body, the large breasts, and the round belly)*

STELLA   He's been whipping you again, that goddamn sadist you go to on Thursdays.

MONROE   I could screw you any time. It's only that loud-voiced bitch on the bed that makes me nervous. I could screw you any amount of times. I'm not queer at all. It's a goddamn lie that Stella goes around telling just because I don't want to get between her legs and be her little lap dog.

(MIKAELA *laughs and lies down on her stomach at the foot of the big bed.* STELLA *answers her laugh with a shriek. They are both high)*

ABEL   Here?

(Their faces turn toward him, where he sits half hidden by the door. He has leaned back, rocking in the rickety armchair. His hat is on the floor)

MONROE   What do you mean, here?

ABEL   You said you could screw Mikaela any time. Do it *now.*

STELLA *(Shrieking with laughter)*   Oh, you're that sort!

MONROE   Sure, if you like. But if you think you're going to watch for nothing, you're mistaken.

MIKAELA   Come on, Monroe. Let's show them what you're made of.

STELLA   I'm going to bet on this.

(She reaches for her purse, which she has hung on one of the bedposts, and tosses a wad of bills in MONROE's *face.* ABEL *empties his pockets and holds up the money)*

ABEL   Well, how about it? You'll be a rich man, Monroe.

(He throws the money across the floor, gets up, and goes over to MIKAELA, *who is talking all the time to herself)*

MIKAELA   Now I feel fine; now it's just great; now Monroe can come after Major Himmler, who came after Dr. Feuer, who came after Inspector General Wagner. After that I don't know. It doesn't matter anyway. it's been just as usual. Come on, Monroe, before it wears off. I feel just fine. You can take all the money, both Stella's money and the money from that guy who won't tell us his name.

*(*MONROE *has climbed onto the bed. He is still wearing the orange-colored jacket that is too big for him. His slender neck is tense and he is masturbating)*

*(*STELLA *giggles)*

MIKAELA   Quiet now. It's not fair to laugh at him. I'll help him.

STELLA   No, you damn well don't! That's cheating. He must do it himself.

(MONROE *is working away frantically, his chest shiny with beads of sweat. Then he lies on top of* MIKAELA *and tries with his hand to slip his drooping penis in. He squeezes her breasts and kisses her shoulders and neck, making futile attempts to reach her.* MIKAELA *holds one hand to her mouth, leaning her head backward and meeting* ABEL*'s eyes in giggling complicity. Now and then she takes a puff at her cigarette.* STELLA *has crawled up to them and kneels, waving her arm up and down like a wrestling referee. Suddenly* MONROE *collapses over* MIKAELA*'s white, spread-out body, sobbing convulsively.* STELLA *gives a shout and slaps him on the bottom, then throws herself on the floor and begins to snatch up her money.* ABEL *falls over her heavily and she turns onto her back)*

30

A few hours later ABEL *wakes up. The thin woman is lying beside him in bed. Her mouth is wide open and her eyelids have a bluish tinge; she looks dead but is snoring loudly.* MONROE *is lying on the floor with his orange jacket under his head. He is wrapped in a tattered blanket that leaves his skinny legs and big, flat feet sticking out. He is dead to the world, sleeping off the effects of a cocaine fix. From the next room a violent argument can be heard.* MIKAELA *seems to be in dispute with a customer.*

ABEL *dresses quickly, puts on his overcoat, finds his hat, and is on the point of tiptoeing out when he remembers something.*

Cautiously he opens the drawer of the bedside table. His money is lying there in an untidy heap. He stuffs it into his pocket with a pack of cigarettes and sneaks out.

The time is three thirty in the morning and the streets are deserted, swept by a cutting wind from the plains to the north. Near St. Anna's Clinic an army patrol is posted; a truck has driven up onto the sidewalk, an old-fashioned machine gun is mounted on the platform, and the seven soldiers comprising the little group are crouching around the truck. Light is shining out through the half-open door of a milk store, and the proprietress is standing by a hissing Primus stove making coffee. The men are sipping the hot liquid from the lids of their canteens; some are chewing crusts of black bread. Sunk deep in their greatcoats, they seek shelter from the wind.

ABEL *goes up to the group and shows his stolen cigarettes.*

ABEL   Cigarettes?

(Some of the men accept)

ABEL   Does anyone speak English?

(Silence, and sleepy, suspicious looks)

ABEL   I'd like to know the way to the Stettiner railroad station.

(One of the men tells him in broken English how to get there)

ABEL   Thanks a lot. Have a cigarette. Take the whole pack. *(Pause)* I'm an American. I'm on my way to Hamburg. My boat leaves this afternoon. I came to Berlin to see what the inflation was like. Fantastic. Then I was with some whores and had my dollars stolen. Oh, well, it doesn't matter much. I had my money's worth. *(Laughs)* Lot of soldiers about tonight.

Anything special cooking? *(No answer)* I'll be glad to
get back to Los Angeles. It's not so goddamn cold there
at any rate. *(Pause)* Anyone got a light? My matches
were pinched, too. The only thing they let me keep
was my cock. *(Laughs; silence)* Though they knew their
job all right, I must admit. Especially one of the girls
—she was Jewish. Jewish girls make good whores. But
you've too many Jews in this town. The place is filled
with them. Do you like Jews? *(Silence)* I don't. All right
as tarts, though. Red-haired Jews make me want to
throw up.

(Silence. Someone hands ABEL *a tin mug of coffee. He thanks
the man with a smile. Tears come to his eyes. He sips the coffee
and smokes)*

ABEL   I'll be glad to get home to a warm climate. And to
my wife and kids. As the tarts stole my wallet, I can't
show you any photos of the family. We don't live in
Los Angeles itself but on a hill by the ocean. The
Pacific Ocean. We wake up and fall asleep to the sound
of the surf. Nearly every day of the year we go down
to the beach for a swim. My wife has a nice figure. It
shows off well in a swimsuit. We have two kids, Max
and Manuela. The girl starts school next fall. My old
grandma lives with us. She's an old bitch really, but
she does the housekeeping and the kids love her.
What's more, she's a marvelous cook. You should just
taste her apple pie.

SOLDIER   Oh, go to hell!

ABEL   *(Laughing)*   What have I done to offend him?
Maybe he's a Jew. In that case, you have a traitor in
your midst.

SOLDIER Scram before I shoot you.

ABEL *(Showing the wad of bills)* Maybe you'll let me pay my whack.

(He stuffs the money into the pocket of the soldier nearest him)

ABEL Good-bye, gentlemen. For your sake, I hope Germany's still here on Thursday. I wouldn't bet on it if I were you.

31

When ABEL *gets home he undresses quietly in the cold hall and tiptoes into the room. The ceiling light is on.* MANUELA *is lying in bed with her arms stretched by her sides. Her head is turned to the wall, and she has vomited on the pillow. When he comes nearer he sees that her eyes are wide open and that she is dead.*

There is silence all around him. He sees the body's unreality, illuminated by the bleak light from the ceiling. He sees the brooding darkness outside the windows. To get away from all this he shuts his eyes and breathes deeply, trying to deaden the pain in the slow movement of breathing. There are no tears left.

He is roused by a faint noise behind the wall. He seems to see a sudden reflection of light inside the tall, gold-framed mirror beside the wardrobe. On an impulse he seizes one of the chairs and with all his might, dashes it through the glass, which shatters inward, leaving a gaping hole. For a moment he stands amazed and frightened, then he hears quick footsteps and a door being slammed. He climbs onto another chair and focuses the ceiling light on the opening. In the dark beyond it something is gleaming. It looks like a staring eye. When ABEL *shines the light closer on the mysterious object, he sees that it is a film camera with the lens turned toward his face. He knocks out the jagged bits of glass left in the frame and, creeping through the hole, pushes the camera over. The cassette flies open and the film coils out over the floor like a yellowish snake. He shoves open a door and finds himself in a large, unfurnished room with tall windows and pulled-up floorboards, which expose underlying joists and, between them, a bottomless abyss. The gilt leather lining the walls is peeling off, and the four windows are bare against the black of the night. Some steep wooden stairs lead to an upper floor and another door. Beyond it everything is painted white, the walls are tiled, and the windows nailed up. In the middle of the floor stands an operating table; otherwise the room is empty, as if all the furniture and fittings had been removed in great haste. The next door: a big elevator for the transport of goods. He presses a button and a motor begins to hum, vibrating through floors and walls. The elevator starts, carrying him up through the dark house, lighted here and there by a naked bulb. Traces of hasty departure everywhere. The elevator stops at the top floor and* ABEL *is standing in a corridor that seems to stretch the entire length of the house. Half-open doors everywhere, and rubbish that has been left behind.*

Suddenly a shadow comes toward him. ABEL *glimpses a sallow face, a pair of cold, glittering eyes, a tight mouth. He flings himself to one side and the attacker falls.* ABEL *takes to his heels. He finds a staircase and rushes down it. He is pursued. Now he is standing in a basement room and in front of him is the elevator shaft, gaping upward and downward. There is no gate in the grille. The pursuer has caught him, faceless in the gray, indirect light from an opening below the ceiling.* ABEL *tries to escape, but the pursuer presses him against the grille and the operating buttons of the elevator shaft. The motor starts, walls and floor vibrate faintly with the hum, and the elevator moves slowly downward. They fall; the attacker is on top of* ABEL *and bangs his head against the floor. The elevator comes closer.* ABEL *braces himself and pushes them both inward toward the black hole of the shaft. The man flinches for a moment and lets go.* ABEL *pulls him down and holds him by the shoulders, pressing him against the floor, with the man's head hanging over the shaft. The elevator passes close against* ABEL*'s face.*

32

DR. SOLTERMANN *stands looking at his pocket watch, which he is slowly winding up with a tiny key attached to a thin, gold chain. The childlike blue eyes are cold and the former familiarity is gone. He smiles without smiling; the corners of his mouth are pulled aside, exposing a row of teeth that are too white.*

SOLTERMANN When you began your employment, I pointed out that working hours are from eight to six.

(Another smile, which dies as suddenly as the first. A dusty sunbeam penetrates the grimy window and shines on Dr. Soltermann's white hair)

ABEL Would you be kind enough to conduct me to my workplace? I can't find the way.

SOLTERMANN Of course.

(They go through the labyrinth in silence. The old man walks quickly, irritatingly jingling a bunch of keys that he holds in

his right hand. ABEL *follows close behind him. Suddenly footsteps are heard and a door slams.* ABEL *stops)*

ABEL   Are there other people here in the archives?

SOLTERMANN   Of course. Every day we are visited by
scientists from other institutions.

(They come to ABEL*'s room.* DR. SOLTERMANN *stops at the
door and nods curtly, waiting impatiently for* ABEL *to step
in.* ABEL *puts out his hand, grabs* DR. SOLTERMANN *by the
arm, and flings him against the table. He falls to the floor.*
ABEL *bangs the heavy iron door, rushes over, and lifts the
old man up. His glasses are broken and he is trembling
violently)*

SOLTERMANN   You behave most indecorously toward an
old man.

(He smiles again, having managed to control his shaking. He puts down his broken glasses)

SOLTERMANN It's all so absurd and humiliating. Surely you realize I won't tell you anything, however roughly you use me. Unlike you, I have a conviction. Something unheard-of is happening down there in Munich, Herr Rosenberg. A savior is born, but the delivery is taking place through pain and blood. A terrible time is at hand, but what is thirty or forty years of suffering and death? What do you or I matter? What do millions and millions of lives that must be sacrificed matter? There are plenty of human beings, Herr Rosenberg. The slack age of individualism is past. Someone is standing ready to give voice to the suppressed screams, to give words to the mute anguish. Kill me, Herr Rosenberg. I won't resist. My body is weak, but my soul is strong and calm.

*(*DR. SOLTERMANN *has spoken quickly and very softly. Time and again tears well up in the blue, unprotected eyes. He takes out a handkerchief and blows his nose)*

ABEL Give me the keys.

(He puts out his hand for the bunch of keys, but the old man shakes his head and puts it in his pocket. ABEL *takes a step toward him and tries to seize it.* DR. SOLTERMANN *resists, his arm cracks, and he cries out.* ABEL *claps his hand over the old man's mouth, flings him down across the table, and bangs his head against it. The frail body goes limp in his hands at once, the eyes roll backward, and* DR. SOLTERMANN *begins to snore.* ABEL *takes the keys and, having tried several, unlocks the iron door.*

*Corridors and narrow passages extend in all directions.
Without great difficulty,* ABEL *finds the archive where he was
the previous day with* DR. FUCHS. *He listens, but there is
silence all around him; the only sound is the hissing of some
pipes that run the full length of the corridor just below the
ceiling.*

*At one end of the room, wedged behind the shelves, is a low
door.* ABEL *finds a key to this lock, too. He enters a cramped,
square room rather like a large wardrobe. There are no windows. In the middle of the floor stands a peculiar machine: a
table on which two large wheels are erected, with a telescope
between them. On one wheel a reel of film has been wound.*
ABEL *looks around him. Shelves on the walls are full of round
metal boxes. Each box has a marking.*

*On the right of the machine is a square control panel. He
turns on one of the switches. A hidden projection lamp lights
immediately, and a still picture is shown on a small screen
fixed at the end of the table. The picture is of a woman sitting
on a chair by a white wall. Her posture is tense and the
face looks tormented.* ABEL *puts on the other switch. The
two wheels begin to rotate, the film runs through the lens,
there is a rattling, and the picture of the woman begins to
move.*

ABEL *turns around.*

HANS *has slipped quietly into the room. He closes the door,
locks it, and switches off the projector)*

HANS   I have locked the door so that no one will disturb
us. *(Smiles)* Dr. Soltermann warned me against you,
but I didn't believe him. By the way, who would have
thought that Dr. Fuchs would blab? He was always so
afraid. And always saying how much he admired me.
(Gravely) You say nothing. Switch on the projector
again and you'll see some interesting pictures. They
were taken during our experiments here at St. Anna's
Clinic.

(ABEL *switches on the current. The machine begins to rattle again, and the picture of the woman on the screen moves*)

HANS   This is a resistance experiment, unfortunately not fully documented, but as yet our apparatus is far from perfect. A woman of thirty who volunteered to look after a four-month-old baby with brain damage who screams day and night. We wanted to see what would happen to this completely normal, fairly intelligent woman if we shut her in with a child who never stopped screaming. As you see, after twelve hours she is still quite self-possessed.

(ABEL *watches.*
The woman in the picture gets up from the chair and goes over to the cot, where the screaming child is lying; picks it up, handling it with great tenderness; and walks up and down, rocking it in her arms)

HANS   At first, when the woman found we had locked her in with the child, she was very upset. She beat on the door and shouted; but when she realized her situation, she behaved very sensibly. She settled down to make the best of things and survive together with the screaming child. Now, however, twenty-four hours have passed.

(ABEL *watches.*
A text rushes past denoting the difference in time. The woman has sat down in a corner of the room and is holding her hands to her ears)

HANS   We can now see that she is affected. Her sympathy for the sick child has been wiped out by an influence that is too strong for her. Her feelings have been replaced by a deep depression, which in its turn para-

lyzes every initiative. You can see how strangely she
behaves when she eats, crouching down to the floor,
hardly able to chew. She has left the child to its
fate.

(ABEL *watches.*
   The woman is standing over by the baby's cot, her arms
hanging at her sides. Her head is bent and ABEL *cannot see*
her eyes. One shoulder is drawn up)

HANS   Here we can see quite clearly that the thought of
ridding herself of the child has matured. But it took
another six hours before she carried out her intention.
A remarkable resistance. Unfortunately, our camera
didn't manage to document the actual deed. As I men-
tioned, our apparatus is still defective.

(The screen has gone dark, but the machine rattles on.
   ABEL *watches.*
   The picture now shows two men in a white room. One of
them is dressed in a white coat and white pants. The other is
naked and is lying on a wooden table with arms and legs
fastened by leather straps. He is blindfolded. The white-coated
man is holding a thick hypodermic needle between thumb
and forefinger. Now and then he jabs it into the bound
man's body. The victim shrieks; his chest is covered with
sweat)

HANS   This experiment falls into two phases. This is the
first. The subject, who cannot see and who is tied
down, is jabbed with a needle hour after hour at very
irregular intervals. Sometimes five or six slight jabs in
the course of a minute, sometimes with a gap of thirty
minutes. This gradually creates an almost unbearable
panic in the subject.

(ABEL *watches.*
A text flickers past, saying in German that the first phase of the experiment is concluded after ten hours' treatment)

HANS   The interesting part of the experiment comes here in the second phase. The effect ceases after about ten hours. The subject is freed from his bonds. The doctor who has been giving the treatment now talks to him, gives him something to drink, washes him, and helps him to light a cigarette.

(ABEL *watches*)

HANS   The doctor establishes a kind of synthetic affection between himself and the victim, who leans against his tormentor's shoulder, weeping with pain and misery but feeling no hostility toward the man who has been torturing him. On the contrary, he is very responsive to the doctor's artificial kindness. He expresses an affection that is entirely conditioned by the state of shock in which he finds himself.

(*The screen at the end of the table goes dark again, but the machine rattles on. The smell of hot metal rises with the heated air against* ABEL'*s face*)

HANS   You'd like to see more, wouldn't you?

(ABEL *watches.*
A man presses himself against the white wall. It is obviously hard for him to keep his balance. His eyes are wide open and his mouth keeps moving. Time and again he stretches out his arms, as if seeking support. He takes a step but immediately falls down, gets up, and falls again)

HANS   For seventeen days this man has been shut up in
a cell, so constructed that he has not been able to move
either arms, legs, or head. In addition, he has been
deprived of all sound and has been in total darkness.
I know what you're going to say: You're wondering
how we could get anyone to agree to such an experiment voluntarily. No difficulty, I can assure you.
Under present conditions, we have an enormous
amount of material to choose from. People will do
anything for a little money and a good square meal.

*(The picture fades, the screen flickers white, an illegible text
rushes past.*
   ABEL *watches)*

HANS   These pictures are not particularly instructive
but may be of physiognomic interest. The subject has
been given an injection of Thanatoxin, a drug that
produces violent mental pain. What you see, therefore,
is someone subjected to unbearable agony, a total and
indefinable dread. Here you see him just as he is given
the injection. You notice that he is quite balanced and
is laughing and joking. An unusually nice boy, inci-
dentally. He was a student and was reading political
science at the university. We're back now at the condi-
tion of dread, which is getting worse and worse. In a few
moments he'll commit suicide. Watch carefully. It happens without any warning. He picks up the revolver lying there on the table—you can't see it properly;
now you can see it. Then he puts it in his mouth. The
gun is not loaded, of course, but he doesn't know that.

*(The anguished young man throws the revolver down and
falls against the wall. He rolls about on the floor, holding his
head. The picture fades.*
   ABEL *watches)*

HANS   What was I going to say now . . . Oh, yes, that student really did shoot himself a few days later, although the effects of the Thanatoxin had quite worn off. *(Pause)* Your brother, Max, met with the same misfortune. By the way, he was one of our best assistants.

(ABEL *looks at Hans in silence*)

HANS   He was intelligent and, what is more, was really interested in our experiments. He himself wanted to try out the Thanatoxin. I advised him not to, but he insisted. His fiancée also helped us quite a bit. They were very attached to each other and lived for a time in one of the apartments that you yourself . . .

(The heavy machine clatters on inexorably and now shows a room furnished more or less like ABEL *and* MANUELA*'s.*
   ABEL *watches.*
   A man and a woman are having a violent argument. After a few moments they come to blows, striking out at each other in savage fury)

HANS   This is one of our most recent and interesting experiments. Both have undergone an operation. We have inserted two very small membranes in the brain of each of the subjects. One membrane is connected to the center of aggression, the other to the center of sexual activity. Outside the experiment room we have a transmitter that acts now on one membrane, now on the other. From our control panel we can therefore influence the subjects' behavior with regard to aggression and sexuality. Unfortunately, the pictures are not very clear, although we used several cameras. Here you see the actual control panel, consisting of two units, one for the man and one for the woman. Now we influence their sexuality—see how they suddenly change from wild fighting to caressing each other and then to intercourse. During coitus we activate the female partner's aggressiveness. She hits out in fury while the man, who is still under the influence of the sexual stimulation, tries in vain to get at her. It's almost like a farce—at times one can hardly help laughing.

*(The picture changes.
ABEL watches)*

HANS Maybe you're wondering what my intentions were with you and Manuela, placing you as I did in one of our experiment rooms and giving you food from the diet kitchen. Will you believe me if I say that I had no intentions at all? I wanted to help you. The food you received was never tampered with. It was merely a little better than the ordinary hospital fare. As you saw, the building had been vacated. Some time ago we were forced to transfer our activities to a more out-of-the-way place. We must take great care, as you will realize. Moreover, our economic resources are limited—we are financed entirely by private means. *(Smiles)* I'm not a monster, Abel. What you have seen are the first faltering steps of a necessary and logical development.

(He is silent and lights a cigarette. The machine clatters on, now showing a series of faces—people moving along a wide street in the dusk)

HANS The second you open that door you'll be killed. I know that you've told Inspector Bauer of your experiences. I know, too, that justice, represented by the stupid and good-natured inspector, has begun to move, slow and creaking. In a moment he'll be here with his police and his rusty guns. In a few minutes I'll bite on a cyanide capsule that is now inside my right cheek. I did consider burning the archives and destroying the results of our work, but it seemed too melodramatic. The law will take charge of our results and study them, and then the law will file them. In a few years' time, science will ask for the documents to be brought out and will continue to build on our experiences on a gigantic scale. *(Pause)* We're ahead of our time, Abel. We must be sacrificed. It's only logical. *(Pause; then he smiles)* In a day or two, maybe even tomorrow, the national units in southern Germany will attempt a revolt, led by an incredible scatterbrain named Adolf Hitler. It will be a colossal fiasco. Herr Hitler lacks intellectual capacity and every form of method. He doesn't realize what tremendous forces he is about to conjure up. He will be swept away like a withered leaf the day the storm breaks. Abel, look at that picture.

Look at all those people. They're incapable of a revolution—they're far too humiliated, too afraid, too down-
trodden. But in ten years, the ten-year-olds will be
twenty, the fifteen-year-olds will be twenty-five. To
the hatred inherited from their parents they will add
their own idealism and their own impatience. Someone will step forward and put his unspoken feelings
into words; someone will promise a future; someone
will make demands; someone will talk of greatness and
sacrifice. The young and inexperienced will give their
courage and their faith to the tired and the vacillating,
and *then* there will be a revolution and *our* world will
go down in blood and fire. *(Pause; he sits down)* In ten
years, not more, those people will create a new society
unequaled in world history.

*(ABEL switches off the machine; it stops and goes out. He goes
to the door and tries it. It is locked, and the key has been taken
out. He leans against one of the shelves, staring with tired,
aching eyes at HANS, who is sitting back comfortably, toying
with a rusty pair of scissors)*

HANS   The old society, Abel, was based on extremely
romantic ideas as to man's goodness. It was all very
complicated, since the ideas didn't correspond to the
reality.

(ABEL looks at him)

HANS   The new society will be based on a realistic assess-
ment of man's potentialities and limitations.

(ABEL looks at him)

HANS   Man is a misconstruction. A perversity of nature.
That is where our experiments come in, modest

though they are as yet. We deal with the basic construction and reshape it. We set free the productive forces and channel the destructive ones. We exterminate what is inferior and increase what is useful. The only way to prevent the final catastrophe. *(Smiles)* Do you know what gave us the most trouble with these experiments? Well, I'll tell you, Abel. It was getting rid of the bodies, covering up our tracks. Dr. Eichenberg designed an incinerator to be driven by electricity, but we couldn't afford to build it. The two men on guard out there in the archives, whom Bauer's police will shoot in a few minutes, have had heavy work, but their ingenuity has been impressive. The police have had forty-six murders and suicides to solve. A comparatively small percentage if you think that we have used over three hundred subjects who have returned to their homes oblivious of what they have been through. But the dead ones were a great encumbrance.

(Shots are fired out in the archives. There are screams and shouts of command, then an abrupt silence. HANS *listens with only half an ear)*

HANS I always liked you and Manuela. *(Smiles)* She showed me an affection, which I think was sincerely meant. Against my better judgment I tried to help you. Comic, isn't it, Abel?

(Someone pounds on the iron door and shouts that it's the police and that they'll break the door down if it isn't opened)

HANS If you have understood anything of what I've been saying the last few minutes, you can tell whoever is willing to listen. No one will believe you.

Despite the fact that anyone who makes the slightest
effort can see what is waiting in there in the future. It's like a serpent's egg. Through the thin membranes you can clearly discern the already perfect
reptile.

(The door begins to give. HANS *shuts his eyes and his face
contorts in violent pain)*

HANS   I thought it would be much quicker. I didn't
think . . . it would hurt so much.

*(The door is flung open and two policemen tumble in, guns
in hand.* BAUER *is at their heels.* HANS *has slipped down out
of the chair and his head strikes the floor.*
   A policeman grips ABEL*'s arm. He wrenches it free but is
struck unconscious by a violent blow in the face)*

33

ABEL *comes to in a whitewashed room with no windows. A
white-clad figure approaches, bends over him, and goes away. He
tries to sit up, but his head sinks back on the pillow. A door that
he cannot see is opened and someone comes up to him. It is*
BAUER.
   *He sits down at the foot of the bed, takes his time lighting a
cigar, and nods to* ABEL, *who again tries to lift his head.*

BAUER   You were given a dose of Veronal. You have
slept for two days.

ABEL   What day is it?

BAUER   It's the evening of November eleventh. You are in the infirmary of the central prison.

ABEL   Can I have some water?

(BAUER *helps him to sit up, gives him some water, then puts the tin mug down on the table attached to the wall*)

BAUER   I have been in touch with Hollinger. He thinks he has use for you. The German state will pay for a train ticket to Basel, where the circus will be for the

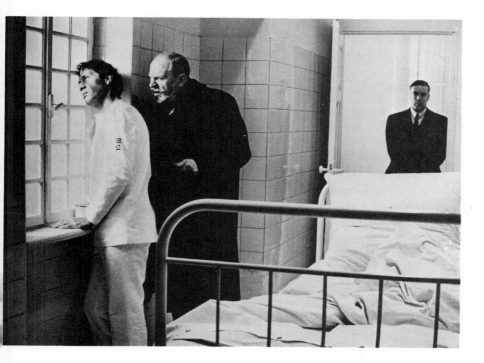

next two weeks. I take it for granted that you will accept his kind offer.

ABEL   I think so.

BAUER   It will be the simplest, Herr Rosenberg.

(He gets up and goes to the door, then turns around)

BAUER   A constable will go with you to the station. The night train leaves at eleven twenty.

ABEL   Thank you.

BAUER   If by any chance you begin to reflect over what you have been through, you can with good reason tell yourself that it must have been just a lot of muddled dreams. Eh, Herr Rosenberg?

ABEL   Yes.

BAUER   We have taken care of Manuela, your sister-in-law.

ABEL   Have you buried her?

BAUER   Buried?

*(*ABEL *is silent)*

BAUER   She has been taken to a mental clinic. The doctors think it will be a long time before she can be discharged. Unfortunately, she is in a very bad way.

*(*ABEL *says nothing)*

BAUER　Good-bye, Herr Rosenberg. *(Turns to go but checks himself)* By the way, Herr Hitler failed with his Munich *Putsch.* In fact, the whole thing was a colossal fiasco. Herr Hitler and his gang underrated the strength of the German democracy. Good-bye.

(He closes the door. ABEL *sits up, stands on the floor, takes a few tottering steps, supports himself against the white wall, puts out his hand, groping in front of him and nearly losing his balance. He behaves like the subject of* HANS *'s experiment who had been shut in for seventeen days, prevented from moving, and deprived of sound and light)*

ABOUT THE AUTHOR

Ingmar Bergman has been one of Europe's leading film and theater directors for thirty years. The first of his films to be known in America was *The Seventh Seal*, which was followed by such great films as *Smiles of a Summer Night, Persona, The Virgin Spring, Through a Glass Darkly, Cries and Whispers, Scenes from a Marriage*, and, most recently, *Face to Face*.

Bergman has received every major American and European film prize and is considered by many to be the world's greatest living film director.